The
iPod
Doing cool stuff with the iPod
and the iTunes Music Store **Book**

Scott Kelby

The iPod Book

The iPod Book Team

TECHNICAL EDITORS
Terry White
Polly Reincheld

COPY EDITOR
Richard Theriault

PRODUCTION EDITOR
Kim Gabriel

PRODUCTION MANAGER
Dave Damstra

COVER DESIGN AND
CREATIVE CONCEPTS
Felix Nelson

SITE DESIGN
Fred Maya

PUBLISHED BY
Peachpit Press

Copyright © 2005 by Scott Kelby

FIRST EDITION: February 2005

All rights reserved. No part of this book may be reproduced or transmitted in any form, by any means, electronic or mechanical, including photocopying, recording, or by any information storage and retrieval system, without written permission from the publisher, except for inclusion of brief quotations in a review.

Composed in Myriad, Lucida Grande, and Helvetica by NAPP Publishing

Trademarks
All terms mentioned in this book that are known to be trademarks or service marks have been appropriately capitalized. Peachpit Press cannot attest to the accuracy of this information. Use of a term in the book should not be regarded as affecting the validity of any trademark or service mark.

iTunes, Macintosh, and Mac are registered trademarks of Apple Computer. Windows is a registered trademark of Microsoft Corporation.

Warning and Disclaimer
This book is designed to provide information about iPods. Every effort has been made to make this book as complete and as accurate as possible, but no warranty of fitness is implied.

The information is provided on an as-is basis. The authors and Peachpit Press shall have neither liability nor responsibility to any person or entity with respect to any loss or damages arising from the information contained in this book or from the use of the discs or programs that may accompany it.

ISBN 0-321-33674-7

9 8 7 6 5 4 3 2

Printed and bound in the United States of America

www.peachpit.com
www.scottkelbybooks.com

For my good friend and
world-class editor, Richard Theriault,
for always making me appear
much smarter than we both know I am.
–SCOTT KELBY

Acknowledgments

Although only one name appears on this book's spine, it takes a large, dedicated team of people to put a book like this together. Not only did I have the good fortune of working with such a great group of people, I now get the great pleasure of thanking them and acknowledging their hard work and dedication.

First, I'd like to thank my wonderful, amazing, hilarious, fun-filled, and loving wife, Kalebra. You're the best thing that's ever happened to me—you're part wonderwoman, part supermom, part business exec, and part standup comic, and every day you manage to put a smile on my lips and a song in my heart. Your spirit, warmth, beauty, patience, and unconditional love continue to prove what everybody always says—I'm the luckiest guy in the world.

I also want to thank my 8-year-old son, Jordan. I'm so proud of him, so thrilled to be his dad, and I love watching him turn into the wonderful "little man" he is becoming. He has so many of his mother's special gifts, especially her boundless heart, and it's amazing the amount of joy he and his mom bring into my life. I'm very grateful God has blessed me with them.

Thanks to my big brother Jeff for all the wonderful things you've done for me (and for other people) and for having so much of our dad in you. Your humor, generosity, and compassion are an inspiration. I love you, man.

Special thanks to one of my very best friends, Terry White. If there's anybody who knows more about the iPod and iTunes, I've yet to meet him, and that's why I had to have Terry tech edit this book. He did an amazing job (as expected), and his ideas, input, and suggestions made this a far better book than it would have been otherwise. I owe ya big time T-bone! (By the way, don't call him T-bone. He hates it. That's why I call him T-bone.)

A very special thanks to my good friend and long-time editor Richard "Dicky" Theriault, who has been editing my books for the past six years, and my magazine columns for years before that. Your friendship has meant so much to me and my family over the years, and working with you is equally as much fun as it is an honor. You've won a legion of fans within our KW Media Group family, and that, along with a hundred other reasons, is why I dedicated this book to you.

Also, my thanks to Polly Reincheld (perhaps Shania Twain's No. 1 fan), who worked closely with me in the development of this book. Her many contributions made this book much easier to write (and much easier to read), and I'm very thankful she's joined our team.

Thanks to my brilliant creative director Felix Nelson, for once again lending his creative ideas and input, which make every book we do that much better.

To my best buddy and book-publishing powerhouse Dave Moser (also known as "the guiding light, force of nature, miracle birth, etc."), for always insisting that we raise the bar and make everything we do better than anything we've already done.

Much love to my amazing creative team at KW Media Group: Chris Main, Barbara Thompson, Daphne Durkee, Dave Damstra, Mary Laurinaitis, Kim Gabriel, Christine Edwards, Bruce Bicknell, Fred Maya, Jodi Nizin, Brett Nyquist, Dave Korman, Ronni O'Neil, and Margie from New York. You guys rock! (Plus, many of you have shown great humility and class when losing to my Fantasy Football team, the "Oldsmar Thunder," and you should be commended. Now everybody, sing the Thunder fight song with me: "We hail thee Oldsmar Thunder. Our hearts are filled with pride. With voices strong....")

I couldn't do any of this without the help and support of my wonderful assistant, Kathy Siler, who keeps kickin' butt despite the string of losses by her beloved Redskins. Hey, look at the bright side—you'll get a first round draft pick, right? (I'm going to pay for that one.)

Thanks to my good friends and business partners, Jim Workman and Jean A. Kendra, for their support and enthusiasm for all my writing projects.

I owe a debt of gratitude to my friends at Peachpit Press, especially my publisher Nancy Ruenzel. They really "get it," and their philosophy and vision make writing books an awful lot of fun, which is very rare in this industry. Also my thanks to Scott Cowlin and Rachel Tiley, who are tirelessly finding an audience for my books.

Thanks to my mentors whose wisdom and whip-cracking have helped me immeasurably throughout my life, including John Graden, Jack Lee, Dave Gales, Judy Farmer, and Douglas Poole.

Thanks to the whole team at KW Media Group, for their commitment to excellence, for refusing to accept limitations, and for being an example of what's best about this industry.

And most importantly, an extra special thanks to God and His son Jesus Christ for always hearing my prayers, for always being there when I need Him, and for blessing me with such a wonderful life and such a warm, loving family to share it with.

About the Author

Scott Kelby

Scott is Editor-in-Chief and Co-Founder of *Photoshop User* magazine, Editor-in-Chief of Nikon's *Capture User* magazine, and Editor-in-Chief of *Mac Design Magazine*. He is President of the National Association of Photoshop Professionals (NAPP), the trade association for Adobe® Photoshop® users, and President of KW Media Group, Inc., a Florida-based software education and publishing firm.

Scott is author of more than 20 books on digital imaging and technology, including the best-selling books *Photoshop CS Down & Dirty Tricks* and *The Photoshop CS Book for Digital Photographers*, and he's the creator and Series Editor for the *Killer Tips* series from New Riders Publishing. Scott has authored several best-selling Macintosh books, including *Mac OS X Panther Killer Tips* and the award-winning *Macintosh: The Naked Truth*, both also from New Riders, and *Mac OS X Conversion Kit: 9 to 10 Side by Side* from Peachpit Press.

Scott is Training Director for the Adobe Photoshop Seminar Tour, Conference Technical Chair for the Photoshop World Conference & Expo, and a speaker at graphics trade shows and events around the world. He is also featured in a series of Adobe Photoshop training videos and DVDs, and has been training Adobe Photoshop users since 1993.

For more background on Scott, visit www.scottkelby.com.

Table of Contents

Chapter Four   57

It's Tricky

Cool iPod Tips & Tricks

Chapter Five   69

Cars

Using the iPod in Your Car

Table of Contents

Chapter Eight

Imaginary Player

Playlists and Smart Playlists

Chapter Nine

Proof of Purchase

Using the iTunes Music Store

Table of Contents

Chapter Ten   171

Tip Drill

Cool iTunes Tips

Don't Read This (just skip right to Chapter 2)

Chapter 2? Why not start at Chapter 1?
Because Chapter 1 is not for you. In fact, I wasn't even going to include a Chapter 1 at all (and simply start the book with Chapter 2), but I was afraid that somebody would buy the book and need Chapter 1 (again, not you, mind you, but someone).

Okay, so if Chapter 1 isn't for you, who's it for? Basically it's for freaks. See, here's the problem: When you first get your iPod, it's basically a brick. It can't do anything because it doesn't come with any songs preloaded on it. Not a single song. Nada. So if you open the box and turn it on, it will have the same functionality as a brick—it will sit there in your hand doing nothing. Most folks (you, me, other non-freaks) understand that there are some things that need to be done before you use your iPod (you have to charge it and either download some songs or import some songs on CDs from your computer; then you have to organize your songs into playlists, transfer your song library into your iPod, learn a few things about how the iPod works, and *then* you have a fully functioning iPod that totally rocks). In short, you have to pay your iPod dues.

But there are people out there (you know who they are) who don't want to pay their dues. They only want one thing—instant gratification. They bought an iPod, and they want to use it now. They want to put the earbuds in, go immediately to the mall, and just "be seen" with an iPod. Oftentimes these "people" wouldn't even have a song on their iPod—they'd just fake it—bobbing their heads as if there really were music playing, but that's risky, because if they run into somebody they know, that person might say, "Hey, cool—an iPod. Can I hear it?" Then they're busted. So to get around that, all they would need to figure out is how to download (or import) just one song into their iPod as fast as possible, without learning anything else about the iPod or iTunes or the iTunes Music Store. Then they wouldn't have to pretend that they're hearing music; they would cover themselves from possibly enduring an embarrassing "moment of silence" with a friend. And they would become very well acquainted with that one song.

Well, that's what Chapter 1 is for—it shows those people ("them") how to do nothing more than quickly download one song and play it. So as long as you're not one of "them," you need to start at Chapter 2 and skip Chapter 1 altogether. Now, you probably know some Chapter 1 people, and when you lend them this book, tell them that they only have to read Chapter 1. They'll thank you for it.

Okay, I get the Chapter 1 thing, but didn't you say "Don't Read This" at the top of the page?
Right. That's because if it said "Introduction" at the top of the page (which is what this secretly is by the way), there's no chance you would read it. None. Nobody reads introductions these days. More people watch C-SPAN than read introductions (if that tells you anything). But the weird thing is, introductions are very, very important (after all, if you hadn't read this, you'd be reading Chapter 1, right?).

Publishing companies have spent millions on researching the "nobody-reads-the-introduction" phenomenon, and the results of that research showed that so few people now read a book's introduction that publishers no longer edit or proofread introductions before they go to press. Want proof? Check this out: neeblick sanbo floppybobo. They have no idea what I'm writing here. "I cood litter dis ting wit typos unt dey wood never no." See what I mean? So basically, it's just you and me here, but if you continue reading this short introduction, I can promise you one thing: After you're done, you'll either say, "Hey, I'm glad I read that" or "Now I fully understand why nobody reads introductions." Either way, you've come this far, so you might as well hang in there for a few more paragraphs. *[Hanging in there is hard to do.—Ed.]*

So do I really start at Chapter 2?
Yes, really.

So what makes this book different from all the other iPod books out there?
There are basically two kinds of iPod books out there: (1) The "tell-me-all-about-it" kind, which tell you everything before you do anything. They include in-depth discussions on compression algorithms and debates about analog vs. digital equalizers; they show things like how to export your playlist in Unicode format and how to dismantle and reassemble your iPod while blindfolded. (2) Then there's this book. It's not a "tell-me-all-about-it"; it's a "show-me-how-to-do-it" book. I show you how to do only the most important, most requested, most likely things you're going to want to do with your iPod so you can start using it now.

So how do I use it?
Each page in the book shows you how to do just one important thing. One topic. One idea. One feature. For example, if you want to have your iPod automatically balance the volume between songs, I show you, step-by-step, how to do exactly that. No big discussions about recording techniques, room acoustics, or why some songs are recorded louder than others—just how to turn the sound balancing feature on. I skip the information overload and all the tech-geek jargon, and I say everything the same way I would if you asked me to show you in person. So, when you want to learn a particular thing about your iPod, just find the topic in the Table of Contents (or the index), turn to that one page, and you'll have the answer you need in seconds. That's what makes it a "show-me-how-to-do-it" book. If at some point in the future you decide that you want to read in-depth discussions on compression algorithms, then you'll go buy one of those 500-page iPod books.

Is the book in some kind of order?
I'm glad you asked that. It's in some kind of order, just not the ideal one. In that I mean it's not in the real order of how you'd actually use an iPod from start to finish. In real life, the first thing you'd do is charge your iPod (which takes about three hours for a full charge), and while it's charging you'd go to work in iTunes (the software that lets you sort, arrange, and even buy music for your iPod), because that's what you need to do before you really start using your iPod. So, really, the book should've been in this order: (1) two pages on charging your iPod, (2) a hundred or so pages on using iTunes and the iTunes Music Store, including how to transfer songs into your iPod, and then lastly (3) how to use your

iPod's features. That would be the ideal way to structure the book, but I didn't do it that way. Why? Because of human nature. When people buy a book on the iPod, they expect to open the book and see a lot about the iPod right off the bat. Seriously, think about it—if you went to the bookstore, picked up a book called *The iPod Book*, and instead of seeing a bunch of stuff about the new iPod you just bought, the first hundred or so pages is on some software you may not have even realized you need; you might put the book back down and keep looking until you found a book that's really about "iPods." Right? Well, I've put too much work into this book to take that chance, so I sold out (to "the man"), and put the iPod stuff right up front in nothing short of a slick, subliminal, mind-control marketing gimmick. I knew you'd understand. Hey, but by reading this introduction, you've now learned the real iPod workflow, giving you (come on, say it with me) "real value in reading this book's introduction." See, I told you this would pan out.

Okay, so if it's not in a workflow order, what kind of order is it in? I call it a "use-a-funkability" order. What that means is that when you get to the iTunes chapters, they're in order by what you'll probably wind up doing first, followed by what you'll do second, third, and so on. So even though the entire iTunes section is technically in the wrong place, the section itself is in the right order. So is the iPod stuff. So is everything else. So being in the right order in the little picture, while still not being in the right order in the big picture, makes this "use-a-funkability" work. Come on, say it with me out loud— "use-a-funk-a-bility." It's catchy.

Is this book for Windows or Mac users?
Both. The iPod and iTunes are identical on both Mac and Windows. However, in the iTunes chapters I give some keyboard shortcuts, and because the keyboard on a Mac and the keyboard on a PC are slightly different, I give the shortcuts for both.

How did you know I wanted all these questions answered?
I've got a telekinetic thing going on. Actually, what I have is beyond that. It's called "tele-funkability." Gotcha! (I just wanted to see if you're still paying attention.)

What's with the chapter intros?
I start each chapter with a short intro. They're as meaningful in the complete understanding of the chapter's contents as the word "use-a-funkability" is to anything. In other words, they're for fun, too. I do that because the rest of the book is pretty straightforward stuff, and at some point, after writing page after page of "click here, scroll to that, insert that cable, etc.," I needed some space to break out a can of my inner funk-a-chunk-a-liciousness. I know, it's hard to believe I get paid for this.

Anything else I should know?
Nah—I think you're good. I do want to offer this closing thought: If after all this, you decide to go ahead and read Chapter 1, I won't tell anybody. Really, there's no shame in downloading one song and playing it over and over again in desperate hope of attracting some attention from the opposite sex (sorry about using the word "sex" in my book, but my publisher told me it will help sell more books). Okay, I think you're ready. Turn to whichever chapter you feel most drawn to. Either way, it won't be long before you've uncovered how to master Apple's iPod—the baddest portable music player the world has ever known. It's funk-a-fab-u-los-oh!

Chapter One

I Can't Help Myself

The Chapter for People Who Must Play a Song Right Now

Okay, just so you know—you're NOT supposed to read this chapter. This chapter is only for people who don't really care about learning how to use their iPod, how to use iTunes, or really enjoy the entire process of "ripping, mixing, and burning" (as Apple once called it). This chapter is for very shallow people who simply just want to play a song, just one song, right now. These people have the delayed gratification quotient of a gerbil, so they wouldn't care about "the right way" or "the best way"—they just want to play a song right now, no matter what. That's why I named this chapter after the Four Tops hit "I Can't Help Myself." Now, when you see that song mentioned, it's usually followed by "Sugar Pie, Honey Bunch" in parentheses, so you go, "Oh, *that* song," because there have been about 20 songs named "I Can't Help Myself." I went with the Four Tops version 'cause I'm about "a hundred," and all the songs I know were written before you were born. But I don't care—you shouldn't be here. You should start at Chapter 2 (as I clearly stated in the book's introduction), and you darn well know it, so if you're here, you get what you get—old cliché song titles from a cranky old man. Now seriously, folks, I mean it—go to Chapter 2 and do this right. It's not too late to start putting your life together and that begins with making good decisions. For example, cut your hair. How are you going to get a decent job with that hair? And take down those hippie beads, and enough with the peace signs, and all that "flower power" stuff....

1

Read This Before You Read ANYTHING!

WARNING: Remember, read this first chapter only if you just bought your first iPod, and you're so excited about it that you just want to load a song and play it right this minute. Otherwise, skip to Chapter 2 and start there. Now, is what you would have learned in this short chapter the recommended procedure? Nope. Ideally you'd charge your iPod while working in iTunes (the free software included with it that lets you organize and transfer music to your iPod). You'd import songs from CDs, download songs from the iTunes Music Store, and then create your own custom playlists (honestly, as you'll find out, this organizing and sorting stage is a lot of the fun of having an iPod). Then, once everything was organized in separate playlists and ready to go, during the three hours it takes to charge your iPod, you'd transfer the songs to it, and then you'd begin playing around with all the cool stuff on your iPod. But if you're reading this chapter, you can't wait three hours. You want to hear a song on your iPod right now (but there isn't one there yet; you have to put one there). Well, this chapter will show you how to download a song into your iPod so you can walk around listening to your *song*. Luckily, no one else will know you're listening to just *one* song, and you'll look approximately as cool as if you had actually done things "the right way." Will loading one song and listening to it now hurt anything? Nope. So why not do it? My point exactly—let's get to it.

Don't Charge Your iPod, Yet

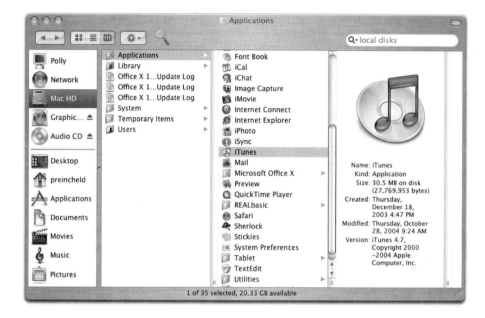

Because in this chapter we're doing the whole "play-one-song-right-now" thing, you can probably skip charging your iPod at this point, because iPods usually ship with enough battery charge to let you turn them on and play a few songs. So skip the charging and instead grab the CD that came with your iPod, pop it into the computer, and install the iTunes software. (*Note:* If you have a Macintosh computer, the most recent version of iTunes is probably already installed on your Mac [look in your Applications folder], so you might as well use that version with your iPod—but if not, just install the CD version.) Okay, that's it for this step—just find iTunes, install it on your computer, and now you're ready to move on to picking your first song.

Picking Your Song

Since you're only going to download one song into your iPod for now, choosing that special song may be a harder decision than you might think. (If you're stuck, may I recommend the song "Ride" by The Vines? Apple used it in one of its popular iPod TV ads, so when you listen to it on your iPod, it'll make you feel as if you're in an iPod ad. I know, that sounds weird, but try it. I guarantee it'll put a smile on your face. Plus, it's a pretty cool song in its own right.) If you don't have "Ride," there's really no sense in going any further (kidding!). Okay, so you've installed iTunes—now what? If you have an MP3 song already on your computer's hard disk, then go under the iTunes File menu and choose Import, then navigate to where that MP3 is on your hard disk and click the Choose button. The song will now import into iTunes, and you'll see it appear in your list of songs. Or should I say, "Your list of song?" What if you don't have a song on your computer? Well, that's the next step.

What If There's No Song on Your Computer (Yet)?

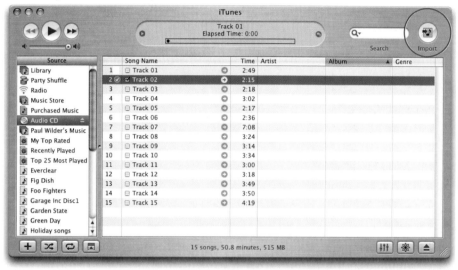

If you don't have an MP3 song anywhere on your computer, then grab a music CD and put it into your computer's CD-ROM drive. The songs on your CD will appear within iTunes (they'll probably appear as Track 1, Track 2, etc., but if you're connected to the Internet when you do this, it may pull the track names down for you automatically—more on this later in the book). So which song do you choose? Track 2. The best songs are never on Track 1. So click on Track 2, then Command-click (PC: Control-click) on the checkbox to the left of Track 2 (or really, any track you want). This "unchecks" all the songs but leaves Track 2 selected. (Note: To hear the song on Track 2, just press the Play button at the top-left corner of the iTunes window). Now click on the empty box where the checkmark had been to designate only that track for importing. When you've found the track you want, click on its box to check it, then click the Import button in the top-right corner of the iTunes window, and that song will be imported into iTunes. You're almost there.

Connecting Your iPod to Your Computer

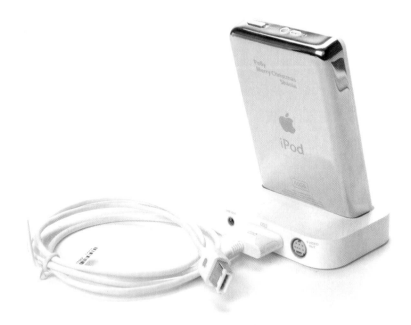

At this point, you have a song imported into iTunes (either from your hard disk or from a music CD), and you're ready to connect your iPod to your computer to begin the transfer. There are two basic ways to connect to your computer: (1) using an iPod Dock, (2) using the FireWire or USB 2 connector that came with your iPod. Docks are great (Docks rock) because they hold your iPod upright (where it's easy to see); they automatically charge your iPod when it's in the Dock; and they make transferring songs a breeze. Now, did your iPod come with a Dock? Here's how to know: Did you spend a ton of money on it? If you did, it probably came with a Dock (high-end iPods, like the 40GB or the iPod photo, come with a Dock included). If you didn't get a Dock, I'd tell you to go and buy one, but we're trying to play one song *now*; so instead use Method 2—the FireWire or USB 2 connector that came with your iPod. Plug one end into the connector on the bottom of your iPod and the other end into the FireWire (or USB 2) input on your computer. Just doing this—connecting this cable—will set in motion the syncing (called "Auto-Sync") of your iPod (meaning the transferring of songs from iTunes into your iPod, so that both iTunes and your iPod are in sync—they have the same stuff). That's it—the song is on your iPod. It's almost time to jam.

Disconnecting from Your Computer

Depending on your iPod's software, you can tell the sync is complete when any one of the following occurs: (1) You see a large checkmark and the words OK to Disconnect on your iPod's LCD display; (2) your iPod's display returns to the Main Menu; (3) the battery icon appears on the display; (4) the iTunes status display along the top center of the iTunes window says iPod Update is Complete; or (5) sometimes a circle with a line through it appears on the display (it will read Do Not Disconnect even though you probably can). When any one of these images appears on your iPod's display or in the iTunes window, take your iPod out of the Dock (or if you don't have a Dock, unhook the cable from your iPod and your computer). Your song is "in there." Now to activate it....

Connecting the Headphones

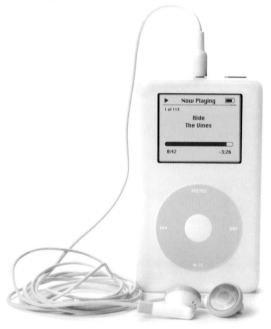

Your song is in there, but to hear it (at this point anyway), you'll need to connect it to some headphones. Luckily, your iPod comes with a set of white headphones (called "earbuds"), and you connect them to your iPod by plugging them directly into the headphone input on the top of your iPod. Just plug 'em in, then put the earbuds in your ears. Did I really have to tell you what to do with the earbuds after plugging them in? I didn't think so.

Waking Your iPod and Playing a Song

By the time you disconnect your iPod from your computer, find your earbuds, and plug them in, it's quite possible that your iPod will have gone to sleep (to save battery life, which is important at this point since you really haven't yet charged the battery). To wake it, press the button in the center of your iPod (you can really press any button, but why not that one, eh?). When you start, you'll be at the Main Menu, so to find your song, gently slide your finger in a clockwise rotation around the center wheel (called the Click Wheel) on the front of your iPod. You'll see the highlight bar move over the various items in your Main Menu as you glide your finger. Stop on Music, press the center Select button, and when the next menu appears, glide your finger along the Click Wheel until you have Songs highlighted. Now you'll see it—your song. Then press the Select button in the center of the Click Wheel and you're there. Press the Play button and glorious audio will pour through your earbuds like music playing through headphones (you didn't expect that metaphor, now did you?).

Pausing, Stopping, Hearing It Again

To stop your song, press the Play button again (so basically, you play and stop a song using the same button). Okay, technically, you're "pausing" the song, but since there's no Stop button, and the song does stop playing, you can think of what Apple calls the Play/Pause button as the Play/Stop button. Want to resume your song from the moment where you "paused" it? Press Play. Want to jump to the end of the song? Press-and-hold the Fast Forward button. Want to hear the whole thing again now? Press the Previous/Rewind button as the song ends. It's a vicious circle.

You Did It!

That's it. You imported a song into iTunes, you transferred that song into your iPod, and you played that song (probably multiple times) through your earbuds. Life is good. Now, you've just scratched the surface of what the whole iPod experience is all about. There are so many cool, fun, exciting, intriguing things you can do with your iPod and iTunes, and that's what the rest of this book is all about—showing you all the cool things you can do that make the iPod the amazing tool (music player, photo player, game player, cool thingy, etc.) that has changed the music world forever. Now that you've gotten that "I've-just-got-to-play-a-song-now" thing out of your system, it's time to "do it up right." So turn the page and let's get to it.

Chapter Two

The Outsiders

How to Work the Stuff on the Outside of Your iPod

I'm not really thrilled about having the word "stuff" in the subtitle of this chapter, but since there really isn't an all-encompassing word that describes all the buttons, sliders, wheels, and inputs on the outside of your iPod, the word "stuff" works as well as any. Okay, what about the title "The Outsiders"? Well, that's a tribute to the 1960s band of the same name, who had a huge hit with the song "Time Won't Let Me," which has been licensed for use in numerous commercials. Considering that this chapter is about how to use all the "stuff" on the outside of your iPod, it's not all that bad a name. Now, how did I come up with that name? It's brilliant, really, but to understand how it came about (and to be there for the actual moment when it all came together), you'll have to read the introduction for Chapter 3. That's right, you have to read another chapter intro, even though by now you've probably realized that these chapter intros have less to do with what's in the actual chapter, and more to do with how late at night it is when I write these intros, and how many glasses of wine I had before writing them. Okay, the last line is made up to make me sound like a sophisticated writer who sips wine, smokes fine cigars, and types by the light of a roaring fire. It's a very romantic version of the truth, which is more like this: It's 9:14 on a Saturday night, I'm sitting at the kitchen table with a half-eaten delivery pizza from Westshore Pizza and an empty can of Caffeine-Free Diet Coke. See, I should've stuck with the wine story.

13

Getting Music into Your iPod

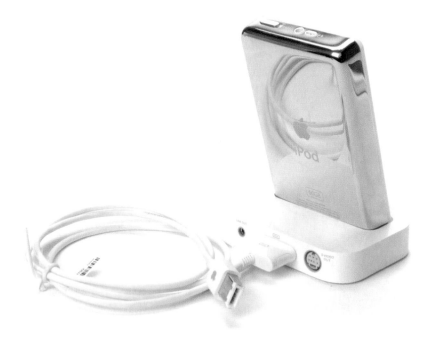

When you've got your songs arranged in iTunes just the way you want them (you've created playlists, put your songs in order, etc.), it's time to get those songs onto your iPod. It sounds complicated, but it couldn't be easier. If you have an iPod Dock, just sit the iPod in its Dock, connect the FireWire cable to your computer, then sit back and relax. The transfer is automatic—your computer will automatically launch iTunes and download your songs, playlists and all. (Watch the top of your iTunes window and when the transfer of songs is complete, you'll see the message: iPod Update Is Complete.) Now you can click the little Eject button (within iTunes) to eject your iPod if you like, but it's not necessary (unless you're using your iPod as a hard disk). Now it's party time.

If you don't have a Dock for your iPod, you can accomplish the same easy transfer process by using either the USB or FireWire connector that came with your iPod. Just connect the cable to your iPod, the other end to your computer, and it'll do the rest. Now you're ready to take your show on the road (so to speak).

CAUTION: If you see that Do Not Disconnect warning, heed it. (*Note:* That's the first time I've ever used "heed" in a sentence. Now I know why—it sounds very "Frasier and Niles.")

Turning Your iPod On and Off

As silly as this may seem (how to turn it on and off), I can't tell you how many people get tripped up by this because there isn't an "On/Off" button. So, how do you turn it on? Press any button on the front of your iPod, and it will spring to life (so, in essence, every button is the "On" button). But it's not that way for turning the iPod off. To turn it off, press-and-hold the Play/Pause button for a couple of seconds and it will turn off. Some people get in the habit of turning the iPod on and off using the same button—they always press Play/Pause to turn it on, and they hold Play/Pause to turn it off. We call these people "sprenger" (which is the German word for "sprinkler"). I don't know why.

Navigating: New iPods and the iPod Mini

*The Click Wheel:
The separate
buttons are gone!*

If you have a reasonably new iPod, an iPod photo, or an iPod mini, you control your iPod using a Click Wheel. There are five buttons on the wheel—one each at the 12, 3, 6, and 9 o'clock positions, plus a Select button at its center. You scroll up and down the iPod's menus by gliding your finger lightly on this wheel (like you're tracing a circle), in either a clockwise or counter-clockwise motion. When you find something you want, you press the Select button in the center. Pretty easy stuff.

Navigating: Older iPods

> Now Playing
> 1 of 113
> Sweetheart
> Frankie &
> The Knockouts
> 0:13   -3:58

> |◄◄   MENU   ► II   ►►|

The older iPod's buttons and Thumb Wheel

Back in the old days (meaning 2001), iPods actually had five buttons (four in a horizontal row and a Select button in the center of a Thumb Wheel), rather than just the single Click Wheel that iPods have today (how people survived this way is hard to imagine). If you happen to have one of these vintage "oldPods," you can still use this book (and lead an otherwise happy and productive life). Just use this decoder: When I say something like: "Press the Select button in the center of the Click Wheel," for you that means: "Throw out your old iPod and buy a new one." Kidding (sort of). Actually, on new iPods and the iPod mini, those four horizontal buttons are gone and their functions now appear right on the Click Wheel (what you call the Thumb Wheel). Luckily, Apple kept the same universal symbols, so if you look at the "oldPod" and at a new iPod or mini, it'll be fairly obvious what to do—you press on the *function* you want, just as if it were a button, and it'll act like a button. So there are no new buttons or no buttons you don't have; they're just in a slightly different place.

Using the Click Wheel and Playing Songs

The Click Wheel itself is stationary—you're doing all the work by sliding your finger (or thumb) around the wheel, or pressing the buttons on the wheel.

The Click Wheel is really more like a touch-pad with a built-in rocker-switch (okay, that makes it sound more complicated than it is). Here's how it works: You touch it lightly with your thumb or finger and gently slide your finger around the wheel in either a clockwise or counter-clockwise direction. So, if you're at the top of a menu and you want to move down the menu, press your finger lightly anywhere on the Click Wheel and start sliding your finger around it clockwise. To move in the other direction (up the menu), just slide your finger around the Click Wheel in the opposite direction. Once you get to a song you want to hear, you can either press the Play/Pause button at the bottom of the Click Wheel or press the Select button in the center—either way, your song will play (hey, that rhymes).

---

iTip

If you're playing a song and you want to pause it, just press the Pause button. Want to resume playing? Press the same button again. (Okay, technically this button is called the Play/Pause button, and if you look at the button, you'll see the Play symbol followed by the Pause symbol, letting you know this button does both, alternately: Play, Pause, Play, Pause....) So if you're playing a song and you want to pause it, press that button. Want to start the song again—press it again.

Fast Forward in the Song

If you want to skip ahead in the current song, press-and-*hold* the Fast Forward button. The key word there is "hold" because if you just press the button once, the iPod will jump to the next song—you have to press-and-*hold* the button.

Not Sure Which Song You Want?
Then Choose Music

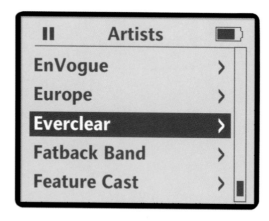

If you're not sure exactly which song you want to hear, then you'll love the iPod's Music feature. Start at the Main Menu, use the Click Wheel to choose Music, then press the center Select button. Now you get to choose how you want to browse: By Artists, by Albums, by Genre, etc. For example, if you choose Artists, you'll see a list of all the artists on your iPod (as shown here). See a group you like? (Maybe Everclear or The Fatback Band?) Just click on the band and you'll see a list of all of their songs that reside on your iPod. It's kind of like a playlist of just their songs. Press the Play/Pause button and it's an Everclear lovefest. You can also browse by Genre (like all Jazz or all Alternative songs), which makes it easy to start playing the kind of music you're in the mood for, rather than having to pick songs one by one. Try browsing this way some time. It rocks (an unintentional pun that should've been intentional).

Done Listening? Don't Turn It Off— Put It to Sleep

If you're done with listening to your iPod for a while, you could turn it off, or you might prefer to put it to sleep by just pressing the Play/Pause button (after a minute or two of being paused, your iPod will go to sleep to save battery life). What's the difference? There are two main differences: (1) When you turn an iPod off (by holding down the Play/Pause button for a few seconds), it turns completely off, so when you restart it later, it starts up from scratch (with the Apple splash screen and all), which takes longer because it goes though a little startup routine. (Note: Your iPod might still remember where you were in a song depending on the amount of time it's been since you turned it off.) (2) If you pause a song and let the iPod fall asleep, when you wake it later it remembers which song you were listening to and where you were in that song; so you can pick up right where you left off (again, this depends on the amount of time you let your iPod rest). So, in short: faster waking and a great memory. It's making me sleepy.

How to Keep from Draining Your Battery

After your iPod is turned off (or put to sleep), before you just go tossing it into your pocket, purse, backpack, computer bag, etc., I recommend sliding the Hold button (found on the top of the iPod) to the "on" position (so the orange part is visible). This locks the buttons on the Click Wheel, so something doesn't accidentally bump into it and turn your iPod on, needlessly draining the battery. If you're really low on battery life, try using the buttons as little as possible (they drain the battery, too). But perhaps the biggest battery-drainer of them all is the screen's Backlight feature, so use it as little as possible and you'll conserve battery life.

Turning on the Backlight

Backlight off

Backlight on

What do you do if you're in a dark, smoky London club on Playlist Night, but it's too dark in there to see your playlists (after all, it's not just dark—it's dark and smoky)? Here's what to do: Just press-and-hold the Menu button and your iPod's backlight will come on, illuminating your screen like a beacon in the night.

Battery Saver: Controlling Your Backlight Time

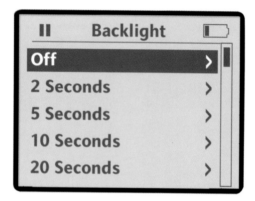

If you really want to stretch your iPod's battery life between charges, this is the first place to stop. If you can get away with turning the Backlight Timer feature off altogether, other "Podders" will envy your longevity. If you can't go "backlight free," set it to 2 Seconds, and you'll conserve quite a lot of battery power. You find this control by going to the Main Menu, scrolling down to Settings using the Click Wheel, and pressing the center Select button. Then choose Backlight.

Updating Your iPod

If you've added new songs to your iTunes playlist (maybe you bought some songs from the iTunes Music Store or imported songs from a new CD), you're going to want to get these new songs onto your iPod. To do that, connect your iPod to your computer (using the Dock or the supplied USB or FireWire cable), and iTunes will launch and automatically update your iPod with the new songs. However, if your iPod was already connected to your computer, this updating won't happen automatically—you have to request an update by (1) going under iTunes' File menu and choosing Update Songs on iPod, or (2) by Command-clicking (PC: Control-clicking) on the iPod icon along the left side of the iTunes window and choosing Update Songs on iPod.

Charging Your Battery (Using AC Power)

When you get an iPod, the first thing you need to do is charge the battery. Luckily, each iPod includes a power adapter that lets you charge it by plugging it into a standard wall socket. Here's how: Take the charging cable and insert the thin flat side into the slot at the bottom of your iPod. Then connect the other end of the cable to the power adapter, then plug it into the wall. That's it—your iPod is charging and you'll see a Charging indicator in the iPod's LCD display.

Charging Your Battery (Using the Dock)

Perhaps the most convenient way to charge your iPod is to use an Apple Dock. The Dock charges your battery using the power from your computer. Not only does the Dock charge your iPod, it's also what you use to transfer songs from your computer to your iPod (using the same FireWire cable). So it's a charger and transfer station in one. If your iPod didn't come with a Dock (they're only included with higher-end models and the iPod photo), you can buy a Dock from the Apple Store or Apple's website at apple.com/store. Once you have your Dock, you just plug one end of the included FireWire cable into the Dock, plug the other end into the FireWire port on your computer, and you're set! (*Note:* If you have an iPod mini, make sure you order the iPod mini Dock, not the regular iPod Dock.)

How's Your Battery Life?

Is it time to charge your battery? Just take a quick peek in the upper right-hand corner of the iPod's screen and you'll see a little battery indicator. If it's solid, you're in good shape. If it's half full, then you're an optimist. (Get it? Half full? Ah, forget it.) Actually it means it's got half of a full charge. If the battery indicator is clear, it means you need to recharge it immediately or your iPod will take a permanent nap.

---

iTip

There's a weird thing about iPods. If you don't use them, they don't hold their battery charge—they just slowly drain. For example, if you've fully charged your iPod photo for a trip that's coming up in four or five days, chances are when you get on the plane, plug in your headphones, and sit back to enjoy your air jams, the battery will be dead. This is a classic case of "use it or lose it." The drain is likely caused by the iPod's internal clock that ticks even while the iPod is off. Also, leaving your iPod in its Dock, connected via FireWire while the computer sleeps, will actually drain the battery. There's no power to FireWire ports while the computer is sleeping.

Replacing Your iPod's Battery

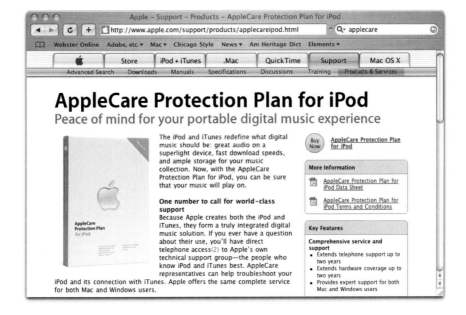

Eventually your iPod's battery will reach the point of no return (it won't hold a charge any longer), and you'll have to get the battery replaced. Well, I have good news and bad news. The good news: Even with lots of use, your iPod's battery is good for at least a year, probably more. The bad news: This isn't one of those "drive-down-to-Wal-Mart and-buy-a-new-battery-for-$4.99" situations. iPod batteries aren't cheap (as of the printing of this book, Apple charges $99 for a new iPod replacement battery), and they should be replaced by a qualified technician (like a tech at the Apple Store in the mall). If you can't spring for the full $99 battery from Apple, you've got a few options. One is to go to PDASmart.com. They'll provide and install a new iPod battery for you for about $68 (plus shipping). Not bad. There's also iPodResQ.com, where for around $79, they'll give you a new iPod battery, do the install, and ship your iPod back to you within 24 hours (the shipping's included). Considering the cost, this is why it's a good idea to get AppleCare for your new iPod for around $59, which would cover a battery replacement if you needed one.

Using External Speakers

Although iPods were born to be used with headphones, they've grown up since then, and now a lot of people are connecting them to speaker systems custom designed for iPods. In my opinion, the two hottest external speaker systems are the Bose Sound-Dock Digital Music System, $299; and the JBL On Stage iPod Speakers, $159 (you can buy either at the Apple.com Store). Both have a built-in cradle (it's like a Dock) that your iPod sits in while playing, and both automatically charge your iPod at the same time. Only one bad thing—although it works with regular iPods and the iPod mini, supposedly neither officially supports the iPod photo. However, I've read that the Bose SoundDock comes with different-sized cradle adapters, and that the largest one does accommodate the iPod photo, but I haven't tested it myself, so....

Chapter Three
Pod's Theme
iPod Essentials

I originally had the idea that I would name the previous chapter "The Outside" because it would cover everything you do on the outside of your iPod (like charging the iPod, connecting it to your computer, and using all of the buttons that appear on the outside of your iPod. Makes sense, right?). Then, I would follow up by calling this chapter "The Inside," because we'd touch on all the stuff that appears onscreen—so basically the stuff that controls the inside of your iPod. It seemed like a brilliant plan, until I realized that the idea absolutely stinks. That's because when people looked through the book's Table of Contents, what would chapter subtitles like "Inside" and "Outside" mean to them? Nothing. Couple that with a chapter title like "The Outsiders" (for the 1960s band), and then it would look like this: "Chapter 2: The Outsiders: Outside." See, it just stinks. Now, if it said "The Outsiders," and then it said, "How to Work the Stuff on the Outside of Your iPod," that certainly would help. Okay, could you please just close your eyes for a moment while I talk to my editor? (Dear Editor: Is it too late to change the previous chapter's name to "The Outsiders?" It's not? Great!) Okay, now open your eyes. Hey, good news! We're going to go with "The Outsiders" for that chapter name after all. But for this chapter, on what happens on the inside—I'm stuck. How about "Pod's Theme" by Lesion? Easy enough—let's go with that (am I saying this stuff out loud?).

Customizing the Main Menu

Unless you've got an "oldPod" (one of those 2001 jobs), you can customize your Main Menu so the features you use most are right there at the top level (reducing your need to dig down through menus). Here's how to customize yours: Start at the Main Menu and scroll down to Settings using the Click Wheel. Press the center Select button, then scroll down to Main Menu and press Select again to see a list of menu items. You can choose which ones you want to appear in your Main Menu by toggling them On or Off using the center Select button.

---

iTip

With the iPod, everything pretty much starts at the Main Menu, and since you'll find yourself going back there fairly often, you might as well learn how to get there fast at any time—just press the Menu button three or four times and you'll be back at the Main Menu.

Rating Your Favorites

I need some music, gimme some more!

Even though you probably have hundreds (maybe thousands) of songs on your iPod, they're not all "your favorite song." Obviously, you like some better than others, and choosing which ones you like best (rating them from one to five stars) can be very helpful in making sure you hear your favorites more often. That's because once you've rated your songs, you can sort them so that your favorites (five stars) play first, then your next favorites (four stars), and so on. (Better yet, you can create Smart Playlists of only your four- and five-star songs—a playlist of just your highest-rated songs, but more on that in Chapter 8!) You can rate your songs in iTunes, or right from your iPod while they're playing. Just press the center Select button twice and the stars-rating window will appear. Scroll the Click Wheel clockwise to add stars—and counter-clockwise to take them away.

---

iTip

If you're rating your songs, it doesn't matter where you rate them—whether it's within iTunes or right on your iPod, because when you next update your iPod, any new ratings (no matter where they came from) are synced between the iPod and iTunes. Your ratings will then be updated in both places automatically, so they're always up-to-date. Cool, ain't it?

How to "Scrub" through the Current Song

Apple borrowed the concept of "scrubbing" from the world of digital video editing, and what it lets you do is quickly jump ahead (or back) to any point in the song while the song is playing. To scrub (while a song is playing), press the Select button once, then slide your finger clockwise around the Click Wheel to scrub forward, counter-clockwise to scrub backward. A black progress bar appears onscreen to give you a visual cue as to where you are in the song (closer to the end, closer to the beginning, in the middle, etc.). When you remove your finger from the Click Wheel, the song starts playing from that point. (*Note:* This feature works differently for an iPod photo. Pressing the Select button only once will show the album art full-screen. You'll have to turn off the album art feature in iTunes to scrub through songs on your iPod photo.)

Getting to Your Playlists

To hear the songs in any one of your playlists, press the Menu button a few times until the Main Menu appears, use the Click Wheel to choose Music, then press the center Select button. Now choose Playlists to see a list of all your playlists. When you find the playlist you want, press the center Select button (but you're not done yet). This displays all the songs in the playlist you selected, but which song do you want to start with? Scroll down to the song you want to hear and press the center Select button again (or the Play/Pause button—either one will do it). Your song will begin playing, and when it's done, the next song in that playlist will play, and so on. (*Note:* If you're an "oldPod" user, you may find Playlists in the Main Menu.)

Shuffling Your Song Order

Once you choose a playlist and start playing a song, the songs will play in the same order you had them when they were in iTunes (so if you had them sorted by length, the longest song would play first, then the next longest song, etc.). That's fine the first few times, but after a while you'll hear a song and you'll already know what the next song is going to be. That's why you'll want to know about Shuffle. It picks songs from your current list in random order—it "mixes things up" so you don't get bored by always hearing the same songs in the same order. To turn on Shuffle, go to the Main Menu and use the Click Wheel to scroll to Settings, then press the center Select button. Scroll down to Shuffle, then press the center Select button to turn Shuffle on (it will automatically choose Songs). If you'd rather shuffle by album (rather than just by individual song), then press the Select button again, and the Songs setting will change to Albums, so two songs from the same album don't wind up playing back-to-back. To turn Shuffle off, press the Select button one more time.

Repeating the Current Song or Playlist

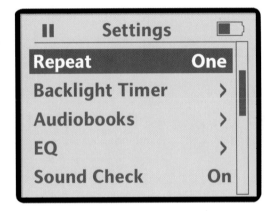

If you're really hung up on a song (like "Hey Ya," which must be heard hundreds of times in succession to really appreciate it), go to the Main Menu and scroll down to Settings. Press the center Select button, then scroll down to Repeat and press the Select button once to repeat only the current song (the menu will show One). Press it twice to repeat the current playlist (the menu will show All), and a third time to turn the Repeat feature off.

Importing Songs Already on Your Computer

If you already have songs on your computer, but they're not yet in iTunes, it will make your musical life much easier if you get those songs into iTunes. Here's how: Launch iTunes, then go under the File menu and choose Import. When the Import dialog opens, navigate your way to the folder of songs on your hard disk, then select the songs you want to import and click the Choose button to import those songs into iTunes.

Which Song Formats Work with Your iPod?

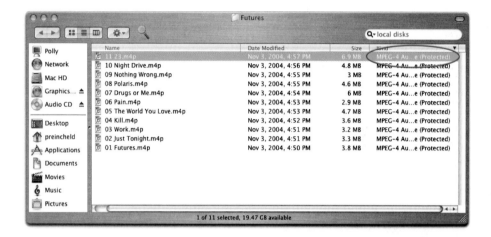

If you're wondering how you can actually fit thousands of songs on a tiny iPod, it all comes down to this—compression. The songs you download onto your iPod are in MP3 format (which is a music compression technique that makes the file size of your songs fairly small, while maintaining nearly CD quality). While the iPod is probably most widely known as an MP3 player, it actually also supports the AAC format, a music format growing rapidly because of its higher-quality sound and smaller file sizes. All songs you buy from the iTunes Music Store come in this new AAC format. (*Note:* There are two AAC formats: the protected AAC M4P, which is encrypted to prevent music piracy; and the unprotected AAC M4A, which is typical of imported audio CD files.)

Finding Out How Much Space Is Left for More Songs

If you're wondering how many more songs you can fit on your iPod, here's a quick way to find out: From the Main Menu, scroll down using the Click Wheel and choose Settings. Then from the Settings menu choose About and press the Select button again to see how many songs are on your iPod, the total capacity of your iPod, and how much space you still have available for songs. To play it safe, you can figure an MP3 song takes up about 4 MB of space (an AAC-encoded song, like ones downloaded from the iTunes Music Store, takes up a little less). So, adding 125 songs would take up only around half of 1 GB. So if you see your Available amount is something like 12 GB, you can load a few thousand more songs and still have plenty of room left.

---

iTip

Another way to know how much room is left on your iPod for adding more songs is to check in iTunes. When your iPod is connected, just click on your iPod's icon in the Source list on the left side of the iTunes window. Then look down along the bottom center of the main window and you'll see a readout that shows how much space is used, and how much space is still free for adding more songs.

Deleting a Song from Your iPod

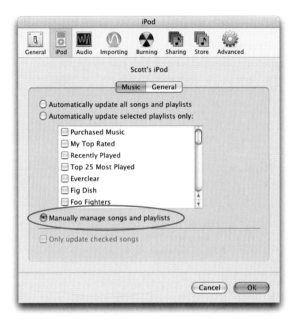

If a song you really hate winds up sneaking its way onto your iPod (this sometimes happens to a song you liked at one time, but after a few dozen plays it really starts to get on your nerves), you can delete it from your iPod. The easiest way is to just delete the song from your playlist in iTunes, then plug in your iPod to your computer. When the iPod updates, the offending song is gone! If you want to do it the hard way, connect your iPod to your computer, then click on the iPod Options button at the bottom-right corner of the iTunes window (or simply Control-click [PC: Right-click] on the iPod in the Source list and choose iPod Options). Then click on Manually Manage Songs and Playlists. Then in iTunes, click on your iPod, scroll down to the song you want to delete, click on it, then press the Delete (PC: Backspace) key on your keyboard. That removes it from your iPod, but not from iTunes.

Creating a Playlist Right within Your iPod (On–The–Go)

Although we normally create playlists on the computer in iTunes, you do have the ability to create one custom playlist from right within your iPod. It's called an "On-The-Go" Playlist (because you're creating it away from your computer), and here's how to create one: Find a song that you want in your On-The-Go Playlist, and then click-and-*hold* the center Select button until you see the song title blink twice (that's the iPod telling you it's been added to your On-The-Go Playlist). Keep adding songs until you're ready to start hearing your new playlist. To find your On-The-Go Playlist, go to the Main Menu, scroll down to Music, choose Playlists, press the center Select button, and you'll find it at the bottom of the Playlists menu. Press the center Select button, scroll down to a song, and press the Play/Pause button. That's it—you're listening to your On-The-Go Playlist. (*Note:* This feature doesn't work if the song is playing. Make sure the song is *not* playing in order to add it to the On-The-Go Playlist.) When you sync your iPod with iTunes, your On-The-Go Playlist will appear in iTunes, where you can tweak it if you like.

Controlling Your iPod's Volume

To turn your iPod up, glide your finger lightly clockwise around the Click Wheel, and to lower the volume (yeah, right), rotate your finger around the Wheel counter-clockwise. The moment you start sliding either way, a Volume Bar will appear so you can see how loud (or soft) your volume setting is, and this bar grows longer/shorter as you increase/decrease the volume.

Enhancing Your Sound Quality (EQ)

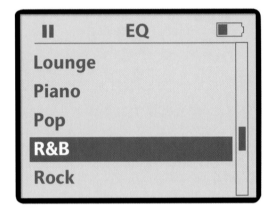

You're about to uncover a feature of your iPod that can make your music sound so much better, you'll never turn this feature off again (and sadly, it's off by default). Your iPod has a built-in sound Equalizer that can change the audio output of your iPod so it sounds best for the type of music you listen to—and best of all, all you have to do is choose from a list of built-in presets. Here's how it works: From the Main Menu, use the Click Wheel to scroll down to Settings, and press the center Select button. Scroll down to EQ and press the Select button again. You'll see a list of preset EQs for each musical taste (e.g., R&B, Hip Hop, Jazz, Spoken Word, Acoustic, Classical, etc., plus special EQ settings that boost the bass, boost the vocals, or reduce the treble). Just scroll down to the type of music you listen to, click the Select button, then go back and listen to your music again. You will be absolutely amazed at how much richer, fuller, and just flat-out better your music will sound.

Saving Your Ears from Volume Abuse

Has this ever happened to you—you're walking down the street listening to your iPod, and a song comes on that's so loud you have to rip the earbuds out of your ears just to keep from blacking out? Thought so. That's because the recorded volume of songs can vary greatly from song to song. Luckily, there's a feature called Sound Check that can come to your rescue. Sound Check automatically balances the volume between songs so you don't suddenly get your ears blasted right off your head. However, this ear-saving feature is turned off by default—you have to go turn it on. Here's how: Go to the Main Menu, scroll down to Settings using the Click Wheel, and press the center Select button. Scroll down to Sound Check and press the Select button to turn it on, which will bring peace and balance to your world (ah, if it were only that easy).

Using Your iPod as a Watch

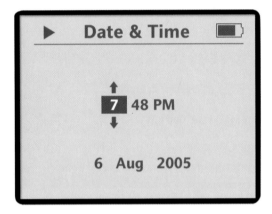

Besides playing music, being your individual PDA, and perhaps even running slide-shows (if you have an iPod photo), your iPod can also function as a clock—and it can even display the current time while you're playing songs. Your first step, of course, is to set the current time. Start at the Main Menu, select Settings using the Click Wheel, and click the center Select button. From the Settings menu, choose Date & Time, then slide around the Click Wheel to set the current time zone, time, and date (you can move from field to field by pressing the center Select button). Once you've set your time, you can have your iPod display the current time while you're playing a song, so press the Menu button until you're back to the main Date & Time menu. Then, where it says Time in Title, press the Select button to set it to On. Now the current time will appear up in your title bar when playing a song.

Setting an Alarm

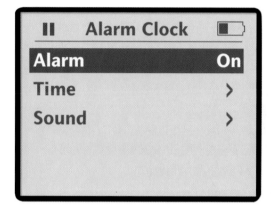

Want to make sure you get to traffic court on time? Use your iPod's Alarm function. Start at the Main Menu, scroll down to Extras, and press the center Select button. Then choose Clock. In the Clock menu, choose Alarm Clock and then press the center Select button to turn on the alarm. Okay, now your iPod's alarm will sound—you just don't know when. So set the time you'd like your iPod to "go off." Scroll down to the Time menu and choose the time when you want the alarm to sound by sliding around the Click Wheel until the screen displays the time you want (this may take a bit of spinning around that dial, so be patient). Okay, your alarm is set. At the time you specified, your iPod will "alarm you" with a beep. By the way, besides just an annoying "beep" you can have your iPod wake you gently with music (or abruptly with music, depending on which song you choose). To do this, in the Alarm Clock menu scroll down to Sound and from that menu choose the playlist and song you want to wake to. (Keep in mind that songs won't be heard unless you have your iPod connected to speakers, though the beep sound will be audible.)

Turning Off the Click Sound

Every time you do something on your iPod (click a button, scroll the Click Wheel, etc.), your iPod makes a "click" sound. This is basically audio feedback so you know "things are happening" when you press something. As well designed as this is, it does tend to drive some people mad (you know who you are). Plus, there are instances in which you don't want anyone to hear those clicks, lest they realize that you're playing with your iPod, when you should be watching the console at the nuclear power plant. So, if you'd prefer "the silence of the Pod," you can stop those click sounds by starting at the Main Menu, then scrolling down to Settings, pressing the center Select button, and inside the Settings menu, choosing Clicker. Now press the center Select button until the option changes to Off. By the way, while you're there you can also designate that the clicks are only audible when you have headphones on; when your iPod is connected to speakers; or you can choose both—all from the same menu.

Is Your Screen Hard to See?
Adjust Your Contrast

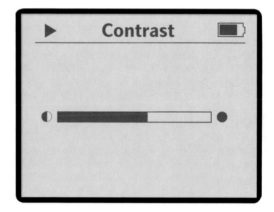

In certain lighting situations (particularly outdoors), you might find that it's hard to see what's going on in the iPod LCD screen, and in bright sunlight the backlight doesn't help much. Luckily, adjusting the display's contrast can usually help. Start from the Main Menu, then scroll down to Settings, click the Select button, then scroll down to Contrast and click to bring up the Contrast slider bar. To increase the contrast (making the LCD display easier to see in bright lighting situations), slide around the Click Wheel in a clockwise motion. To reduce contrast, slide counter-clockwise.

Playing Games

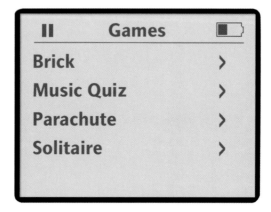

Okay, while it's not exactly an Xbox, your iPod does comes with some decent little games already installed. To get to these little gems, start at the Main Menu, scroll down to Extras, and then press the Select button. In the Extras menu, scroll down to Games and press the Select button to reveal the built-in games. These vary depending on which iPod generation you own, but some of them include Solitaire (this is actually pretty sweet on an iPod photo where the cards appear in color); Brick (a version of the classic "Breakout" game); Music Quiz (just what it sounds like); and Parachute (a lame version of the '80s *Missile Command* arcade game). Press the center Select button to choose a game—and watch the hours just fly by.

Listening to Audiobooks on Your iPod

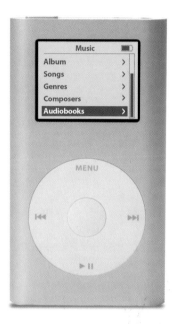

The next time you're taking a trip, you might want to consider taking along a few audiobooks (spoken-word recordings of printed books). These are rapidly growing in popularity, and not only is the iPod designed to play audiobooks, but the iTunes Music Store also sells them. (The iPod also supports audiobooks downloaded from Audible.com.) To find the ITMS audiobook selection, just go to the ITMS homepage and click on the Audiobooks link along the left side. If you find a title you like, and download it, when you update your iPod you'll find your audiobook by starting at the Main Menu, choosing Music, and pressing the center Select button. Then scroll all the way down to the bottom, where you'll find Audiobooks. Click the center Select button again, and your newly downloaded audiobook will appear there. Also, in case you were wondering—when you stop listening to an audiobook, your iPod notes the spot where you stopped, so when you go back to it at a later date, it picks up right where you left off (kind of like a digital bookmark). Better yet, this feature also works in iTunes and in your iPod—even when you sync them, they update each other, keeping track of where you left off.

Renaming Your iPod

If it's time to give your iPod a new name, first connect your iPod to your computer. (Let's say, for example, that you want to change the name of your iPod to "Scott's iPod." Hey, don't laugh. That's what I named mine and I really like it.) Then double-click directly on its name in the Source list (on the left of the iTunes window) and its name field will highlight, ready for you to type in a new name (it's spelled "S-c-o-t-t"). Press the Enter key on your keyboard to make the renaming complete.

Chapter Four

It's Tricky

Cool iPod Tips & Tricks

▶▶ Using a Run-D.M.C. song as the name of a chapter on iPod tips and tricks gets me some props. Some street cred, because no matter how young and cool some of my readers might be, they can't dis Run-D.M.C. because they helped put rap on the map, and rappers of all ages still give them respect. (Notice how I used the terms "props," "street cred," and "dis" in the opening? I did that as a shout-out to my homies and peeps. See, there I go again, using that hip street talk all the kids are using these days.) Look, here's the deal: When you're a middle-aged white guy, all you remember are the slang terms used when you were growing up. Then you start listening to stations like Mix 100.7 and Oldies 104, and you never hear new street slang again. So the old street slang still sounds "new" to you. So, when you're in a situation where you're desperate to sound cool again (as I clearly am here), you instantly revert to words you remember were once cool. Like "props" and "dis." You might even throw in an occasional "chillin'," or if you're really old, you might actually call someone a "jive turkey" (believe it or not, there was a time when people under the age of 18 would use that term [with a straight face], and other people would think they were cool). So now I just sit around listening to old Salt-N-Pepa songs and repeating every cliché ever uttered on early editions of *Yo MTV Raps!* Well, gotta go—my posse's hookin' up with another suck'a crew. (Forgive me.)

Using Your iPod as a Removable Hard Disk

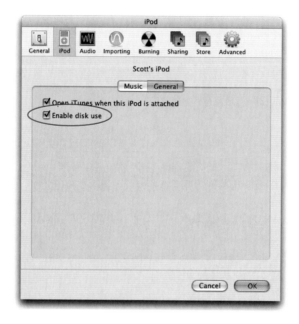

That title is kind of misleading, because your iPod actually *is* a hard drive, so it's not like you're fooling it into believing it's a hard drive—it already knows it. However, for it to *act* like a regular hard disk (where you can store regular data, text files, Photoshop files, videos, etc.), you have to tell it that it's okay to do this. Start by connecting your iPod to your computer, then click on the iPod Options button in the bottom right-hand corner of the iTunes window. When the iPod prefs appear, click on the General tab, then turn on the checkbox for Enable Disk Use. (*Note:* You only need to turn this option on when you have the "auto-update" feature active in Preferences. Otherwise, if you've chosen to update your iPod manually, the Enable Disk Use feature is on by default. See the next page for clarification.) Your iPod will now appear on your desktop, and you can add files by dragging-and-dropping them onto the iPod icon, just like any other removable hard disk. This is great for moving non-music files between machines. There's one thing to remember, though: When it's in this "disk" mode, you have to eject your iPod manually by Control-clicking (PC: Right-clicking) on the iPod icon (either on your desktop or in the iTunes Source list) and choosing Eject iPod in the contextual menu that appears.

Turning Off iPod Auto-Updating

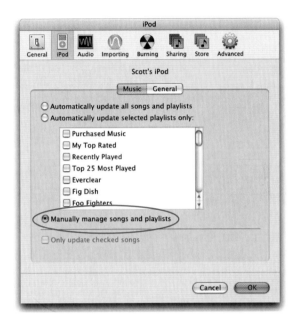

Each time you connect your iPod to your computer, iTunes automatically starts an updating (auto-synchronizing) process that transfers into your iPod any new songs you've downloaded in iTunes, so your iPod is always up-to-date. It also deletes from the iPod any songs you may have removed from your iTunes Library, to keep iTunes and your iPod always "in sync." So, if you're not downloading new songs often, or you're not ready to take certain songs off the iPod, or your iTunes Library is larger than the amount of space on your iPod, you might not want it automatically updating every time you put your iPod in its Dock just for charging—especially since this updating ties up your iPod and iTunes. If you'd prefer to update your iPod manually, you can turn off this "auto-updating." Here's how: While your iPod is connected to your computer, Command-click (PC: Right-click) on your iPod's icon in the Source list on the left side of the iTunes window and choose iPod Options. When the iPod's options appear, choose Manually Manage Songs and Playlists. Now you're in charge of updating, and here's how it works: Look to the immediate left of your iPod in the iTunes Source list and you'll see a gray triangle. Click on it to see all the playlists on your iPod. To update your iPod manually, just drag a song from your iTunes Library (at the top of the Source list) and drop it where you want it into the iPod's playlist. If it sounds like an awfully manual way to update, that's because it is.

Troubleshooting: Your iPod Won't Turn On

If your iPod won't turn on, most likely it's one of two things: (1) Check to see if your button lock (that Hold button on top of the iPod) is turned on. If it is, all buttons are locked. Slide it over so you don't see the orange indicator any longer (which unlocks all the buttons), then press any button to turn on your iPod. If that doesn't do the trick, then go to Plan B: (2) It's probably the battery. Try plugging your iPod into the wall using the AC power adapter. If neither of these two solutions works, try resetting your iPod (using the instructions on the next page).

What to Do If Your iPod Locks Up

If your iPod locks up (meaning, it's on, but you can't get it to do anything—you're stuck on a screen and the buttons don't do anything, the Click Wheel doesn't click, etc.), you can reset your iPod, which will usually do the trick (don't worry—resetting won't erase your songs or playlists). To reset newer iPods (including the iPod mini and iPod photo), just slide the Hold button (that silver button on top of your iPod) over to the lock position (so the bright orange color shows), and then slide it back again to unlock it. Now hold down both the Play/Pause button and the center Select button until the Apple logo appears in the LCD window, then release both buttons. On older iPods, you still slide the Hold button to the lock position and then unlock it, but you press-and-hold the Play/Pause button and the Menu button instead. If you're not sure how old your model is, try both combinations.

Dealing with Hard Disk Problems on a Standard iPod

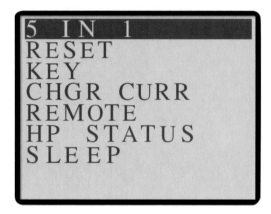

Your iPod stores everything on an internal hard disk, and once in a great while you may encounter an icon at startup that resembles a CD and a magnifying glass. That's the iPod running its own diagnostic check because it thinks something may be wrong. Just sit back and let it do its thing—with any luck at all, it'll fix the problem and return you to your regularly scheduled iPod life. But what if the iPod doesn't think it's sick, but you think it's sick (it's skipping or missing songs or just acting weird, etc.)? Then you can engage the diagnostic tests yourself. Start by resetting your iPod (see previous page), then hold down the Rewind and center Select buttons both at the same time. This brings up a backwards Apple logo. Press-and-hold the Previous/Rewind and Select buttons. Then a menu will appear, in which you can choose what diagnostics to run. If you ever see a mag glass icon with an arrow, that means your iPod detected some problems, and you'll need to run the Restore application to reformat your iPod (this wipes the iPod clean, so make sure your songs are backed up on your computer). Lastly, if you see a sad-looking iPod icon, your hard drive has serious problems, and you'll need to have Apple repair it. *Note:* If you have an iPod mini, you'll see different diagnostic tests. Also, if you have an "oldPod," you'll likely have to use different button combinations.

Your iPod as Contact Manager

You can make your iPod act like a mini-PDA by having it store your contacts (addresses, phone numbers, etc.). If you're on a Mac, and you're using Apple's free Address Book application, it couldn't be easier—just connect your iPod to your Mac, then go to your Applications folder, find the iSync utility, and launch it. Once it opens, go under the Devices menu and choose Add Device (or your iPod will appear automatically). iSync will locate your connected iPod and add its icon to the list of devices available for syncing. Press the Sync Now button, and it will automatically upload your contacts into your iPod. To access these contacts start at the iPod's Main Menu, then scroll down to Extras, press the center Select button, then scroll down to Contacts. When you press the Select button, you'll see a list of all your contacts. Just click on a person's name to display his info. If you're using a Windows PC, it's a little more involved, but it's still easy. Once your iPod is connected, open your contact manager (Palm Desktop, Outlook, etc.) and then drag addresses (your vCards) directly from your contact manager into the Contacts folder on your iPod. (*Note:* To access the iPod's Contacts folder, you'll first have to set the iPod to act like a hard drive, which I covered earlier in this chapter.) Once you've loaded your contacts, you'll access them the same way as mentioned above for Macs.

Putting Playlists in the Order You Want Them

Playlists appear in your iPod in alphabetical order (which makes sense). But what if you want a particular playlist at the top of the list (maybe your favorite playlist)? You can do that pretty easily by pulling an alphabet scam—basically, you just add an asterisk (*) before the playlist's name. For example, if your favorite playlist is called "Wild Nights," you'll just double-click directly on the playlist's name (in the Source list on the left of the iTunes window) and rename it "*Wild Nights." Now that playlist will appear at the top position (but it still won't move above any Smart Playlists). Easy enough, eh?

---

iTip

Wanna know a way-cool secret that Brett Nyquist (NAPP Web Developer and iPod addict) was kind enough to share? If you're jogging, walking, or getting into a fistfight, and you happen to yank out the earbuds from your iPod, the song that's currently playing will pause. All you have to do is plug the earbuds back into the headphone jack and continue throwing punches. Your song will pick up right where you left off.

A Playlist Just on Your iPod but not in iTunes

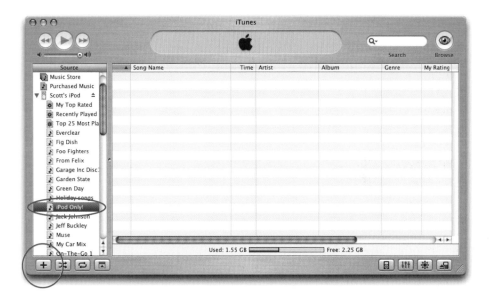

If there's a playlist that you want to appear just on your iPod (maybe it's a playlist you use when jogging, and you never play it in iTunes while sitting at your desk eating a Snickers), you can have this playlist appear *only* on your iPod. Just connect your iPod to your computer, then turn on the manual update feature (covered in Chapter 2). Now click on your iPod in the Source list on the left side of the iTunes window and click on the gray triangle to its left to show a list of the playlists already on the iPod. Now click the Create a Playlist button in the bottom left-hand corner of the iTunes window, and a new empty playlist will appear within the list, with the name field already highlighted (so type in a name, then hit the Enter key on your keyboard to lock it in). Now drag-and-drop songs directly into this "iPod only" playlist, knowing that this playlist will appear *only* on your iPod and won't be adding useless clutter to your regular list of playlists (being the neat freak that you are).

Making Smarter Smart Playlists Using Keywords

Back about a year or so ago, Apple added the ability to embed your own keywords into an MP3 and, because they're embedded, when you move a song from one computer to another, these embedded keywords go right along with the songs. Now, how would you use this? Let's say you're DJ at a party next week. As you go through your songs, you find ones you might want to use at the party, so you can go under the File menu and choose to Get Info on each song. Then, click on the Info tab at the top of the resulting dialog, and in the Grouping field enter your keyword, "Party," and click OK. Then, when it's time to put together a mix for the party, you can have iTunes create a Smart Playlist by choosing New Smart Playlist from the File menu, and in the resulting dialog, choose Grouping from the first pop-up menu; in the second menu choose Contains; and in the text field enter "Party." When you click OK, all the songs with the keyword (Grouping) of Party (regardless of their genre) will appear in your new "Party" Smart Playlist. It makes the Smart Playlist feature even smarter.

Making Sure All Your Songs Are Rated

By now you can see how important it is to rate your songs (especially if you want to make Smart Playlists, and believe me—you want to make Smart Playlists). But you know (and I know) there are songs you haven't rated yet. Well, here's a quick way to find all your unrated songs and gather them in one place so you can rate them. Hold the Option key (PC: Alt key) and click on the Create a Playlist button in the bottom-left corner of the iTunes window to bring up the Smart Playlist dialog. From the first pop-up menu choose My Rating; from the second menu choose Is Less Than; in the stars field click on the first dot to assign the ranking of one star; and then turn off the Limit To checkbox, so it will get all your unrated songs. Click OK, and iTunes will instantly assemble a playlist of nothing but your unranked songs. Start playing a song from that list, and as soon as you rank a song—boom—it jumps off the Smart Playlist. When you're done, connect your iPod, and iTunes will add your new rankings there as well. See, that wasn't as hard as you thought it would be.

Chapter Five

Cars

Using the iPod in Your Car

So you're thinking, "Oh, The Cars—I love that band," but the title of this chapter isn't "The Cars," it's just "Cars," named after the punk rock song "Cars" by Gary Numan. Okay, you're now probably thinking, "The name Gary Numan sounds familiar, but not the song 'Cars.'" That's because the name of the song really should have been "In Cars" (ahh, now you recognize it). Even if you were born before 1980, if I sing a few lines, you'll probably recognize it (from when your parents listen to oldies stations). Here we go (ahem): "Here in my car, I feel safest of all. I can lock all my doors. It's the only way to live, in cars" (Da dunt…da dunt, da dunt). See, I told ya. Now, if I had written that song, I would've used entirely different words. For example, instead of "Here in my car," I would've written "Well shake it up baby now," and when he wrote "I feel safest of all," I would have written "Twist and Shout." Am I crazy, or do my words just sound "right"? I dunno, maybe it's just me. And how about his second line? I mean, come on! Where he wrote "I can lock all my doors," I would've written "Every breath you take," and where he wrote "It's the only way to live," I would've written, "Every move you make." This lyric stuff is easy. Anyway, this chapter is about using your iPod in your car, and all the different ways you can make that happen. What's nice is, once it's connected, you can ride around like I do, coming up with amazing lyrics. Seriously, they just pop in your head. Like for instance, just yesterday I came up with "Here she come now, sayin' Mony Mony!"

BMW Integrated iPod Adapter

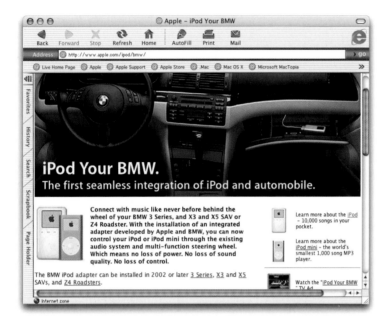

If you're lucky enough to own a BMW, then your life is about to get even better, because so far, BMW is the only auto manufacturer that Apple has "officially sanctioned" to create direct iPod integration. This integration lets you connect your iPod directly (and store it in your glove compartment), and change tracks and volume from your BMW's steering wheel, but there are some—okay, lots of—limitations. First, you pretty much have to have BMW's low-end stereo in your car, because this iPod integration won't work with BMW's fiber-optic-based premium sound systems. If you have a navigation system, you're pretty much out of luck too. Also, although you can have up to six playlists, the playlists have to be named a certain way and can contain no more than 99 songs each. Changing playlists is pretty much out too—and it doesn't display the song names or artists on the BMW's audio system's LCD. So, if you buy a stripped BMW (which is an oxy-moron unto itself), this integration will probably work. Oh yeah, did I mention it doesn't work on all BMW models—just specific ones? (For example, if you own a BMW 5 Series, 6 Series, or 7 Series—I've got bad news.) For more information, visit Apple's website at www.apple.com/ipod/bmw or ipodyourbmw.com or visit your local BMW dealer.

Griffin iTrip FM Transmitter

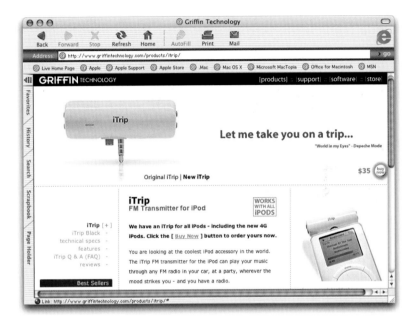

One way to hear your iPod through your car's stereo is to use a wireless FM transmitter, which lets you literally beam the music from your iPod to an FM station on your car's radio. Probably the most popular iPod FM transmitter is Griffin's iTrip, which has three main advantages: (1) It doesn't use batteries, because it draws the tiny amount of power it uses directly from your iPod; (2) it lets you broadcast to any open station, so you get less noise (plus it helps you find that clear station); and (3) it looks cool—and when it comes to your iPod, looks count! They also make a special version for the iPod mini. The operation is pretty simple—it attaches to the top of your iPod (connecting to the headphone jack) and then you're ready to broadcast. Apple sells the iTrip at the online Apple Store, at the Apple Store in your local mall, or you can get it directly from Griffin at griffintechnology.com.

---

iTip

If you bought an all-black special-edition U2 iPod, Griffin makes a matching all-black iTrip FM Transmitter. How cool is that?

Belkin TuneCast II Mobile FM Transmitter

Another choice for wireless iPod FM transmission is the Belkin TuneCast II, which also connects through the headphone jack of your iPod (but it doesn't attach itself like the iTrip). Once connected, you choose a clear FM station on your car radio for it to broadcast to (it can remember up to four clear locations on your radio dial). Besides not connecting directly, there is another major difference between it and the Griffin iTrip: If you don't have a car charger hooked up to your iPod, the TuneCast II requires two AA batteries, which are good for about 10 or so hours of play. So that's the downside. The upside is that it's not just for broadcasting your iPod. You can broadcast about anything that has a headphone jack, including your PDA, a cassette player, a portable CD player, or even (gasp!) another MP3 player. The TuneCast II is available from Apple's online store, the Apple Store in the mall, and from Belkin at belkin.com.

iPod Holder for Your Car—You Need One More Than You Think

There are a few "iPod-in-your-car" options that come with an iPod holder, but most don't; and once you connect your iPod to your car, you're likely to find that the iPod doesn't have a secure home (in other words, it's just sliding around in the car, falling off the console, sitting in an unused ashtray, etc.). Luckily, you have a couple of decent options: One is Belkin's TuneDok, which fits in one of your cup holders and, with its snug-fitting pocket, acts as a convenient home for your iPod. The only real downside is that you lose the use of one of your car's cup holders. It sells for around 30 bucks. *Note:* There are separate versions for the iPod and the iPod mini. You can buy these from Apple's online store, in the Apple Store, or at belkin.com.

Monster iCarPlay Wireless FM Transmitter

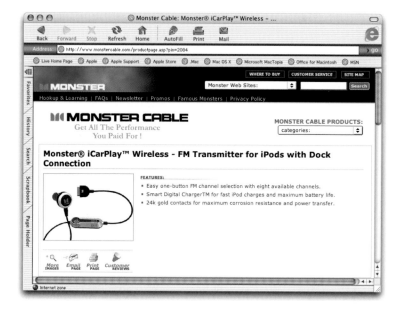

Want yet another choice for wireless FM transmission? Then how 'bout the Monster iCarPlay? This one's also available from Apple's website and their store in the mall. But how does it differ from the iTrip and the TuneCast II? Well, it also charges your iPod at the same time, so not only are you not draining your iPod's battery, you're charging it. Of course, it costs more than either of the other models, because you're getting both a transmitter and a charger, so you'd expect to pay more, right? Also, the iCarPlay only works with iPods that have a Dock connector (you don't need a Dock, mind you—just a connector), so if you have a "Classic iPod" (aka: an oldPod), you're out of luck on this one. Check it out at monstercable.com.

Sony's CPA-9C iPod Cassette Adapter

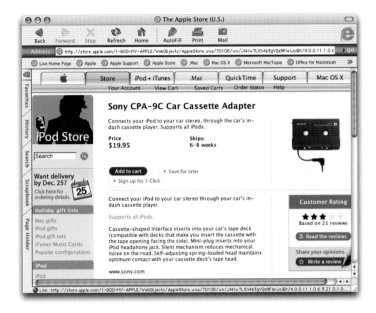

Okay, so what provides better sound quality than FM transmission of your iPod? How about a direct connection using something like Sony's CPA-9C iPod Cassette Adapter (providing your car stereo has a built-in cassette player, of course)? Here's how it works—you pop in what looks just like a cassette, but it contains an input where you connect a line out of your iPod's headphone jack, and now your iPod comes through your car stereo, just like a cassette would. So why the Sony version? Word on the street has it that the Sony just sounds better. Hey, that's what I heard. Apple sells it on its website and in its stores. Best of all—it's cheap—only around 20 bucks. The downside? It's not wireless—you will have a cable running from your iPod's headphone jack to your cassette player, plus you have to have one of those cassette players where the cassette's shorter side is facing outward when you insert the tape, because the connector is on the end.

Dension's ice>Link Plus

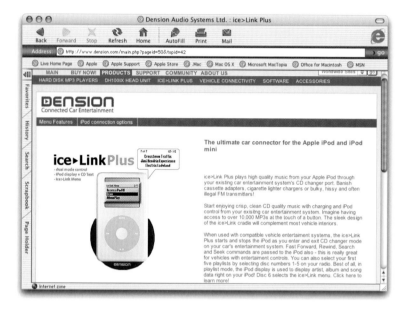

This is probably the closest you're going to get (at this point in time, anyway) to true iPod automobile integration. What it does (if your car model is currently supported) is integrate your iPod into your car stereo so you can control the iPod from the regular car stereo controls (including controls on your steering wheel, if your car has those), and you can change up to five playlists. Here's how it works: It takes over the controls used by your car's CD player, so you connect the ice>Link Plus, press the Track 6 button on your car's CD player, and your iPod is activated. The song titles and artists' names will be displayed on your car stereo display (not even the BMW iPod integration offers that). To get to your first five playlists, just press your CD player's Track 1 button, 2 button, etc. The Next Track button on your car's steering wheel plays the next song on your iPod. Sweet! But this level of integration ain't cheap. ice>Link Plus sells for around $199 to $399, depending on the make and model of your car (and if you have it professionally installed). Visit dension.com for details.

Dr. Bott's iPod Universal Connection Kit II with Tape Adapter

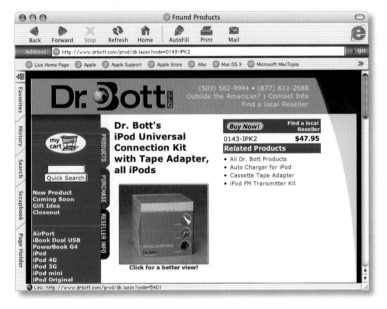

If you're not exactly sure which cables and connectors you need to connect your iPod to your car's audio system, but you do have a built-in cassette player in your car, this may be your answer. Dr. Bott's Universal Connection Kit comes with all the cables you need, including a charger and a cassette tape adapter solution for your iPod. Plus, since this is a "universal" connection kit, you get the bonus of just about every kind of connector to connect to every kind of audio source—not just your car—so you can connect to your home stereo, home cinema, you name it. The kit sells for nearly 50 bucks, and you can find it at drbott.com.

Alpine KCA–420i iPod Interface Unit

If you have an "iPod Ready" Alpine car audio system, you're gonna love this! In fact, if you don't have one, this alone may be reason enough to upgrade your system to Alpine, because with its in-car integration kit (which sells for around $100), you can connect and control your iPod through your Alpine stereo, just like you would a CD player or other audio device. You can even tuck your iPod out of sight in your glove compartment, since it's fully integrated using the Dock connector on the iPod's bottom. You'll see the track name, artist, etc., right on your Alpine stereo's LCD screen, and it even charges your iPod while it's doing it. You can get the iPod interface unit through any Alpine dealer.

If Your Car Has an Auxiliary Input, You're Almost There!

If you're lucky enough to have a car that has an auxiliary input jack, you're about 30 seconds from iPod integration. I'm among those lucky ones, because I have a navigation system in my car, so my car's manufacturer put a small audio-in jack in my glove compartment (the owner's manual says it's for connecting a portable cassette player, since the dashboard space is used by the nav system). So all I had to do was buy a cheap audio cable to run from the iPod's headphone jack out to the input jack in the glove compartment. (If you want improved sound quality and have an iPod with a Dock connector, then you probably should take advantage of the iPod's line level audio output with the din Connector by SIK [sik.com/din.php].) Then I pressed the Auxiliary button on my car stereo, and there it was—glorious iPod through my stereo. I can control the volume from my steering wheel as well, because it's just controlling the overall volume of my car's audio system. I can't change tracks without going into my glove compartment, but luckily a friend (this book's Tech Editor, Terry White) bought me as a gift a Radio-Frequency wireless controller (see the RemoteRemote from Engineered Audio later in this chapter); so even though my iPod is out of sight, I can still change tracks wirelessly. Then, for around 80 bucks I had my dealer install another cigarette lighter-style charging socket in my glove compartment so I never have to charge my iPod's batteries. The moral of the story? Look in your glove compartment for a tiny audio input jack. It could be there, just waiting for your iPod.

Belkin Auto Kit for iPod (Has Line Out)

Whether you wind up using an FM transmitter or an iPod cassette adapter (or almost anything else), unless you get a solution that includes a charger, you're going to need one to keep your iPod charged while you're using it in the car. I personally like the Belkin Auto Kit for iPod because it not only charges my iPod, but also includes a 3.5mm connector so you can connect directly to an FM transmitter or a cassette adapter. It comes with a volume amplifier so you can adjust the volume of your iPod separately. (I know I keep recommending Belkin products, but don't worry—they don't give me any compensation of any kind—every Belkin product I have, I bought.) The downside to this charger? It's a bit pricey at around $40. Apple carries this charger, or you can get it from belkin.com.

RemoteRemote (from Engineered Audio)

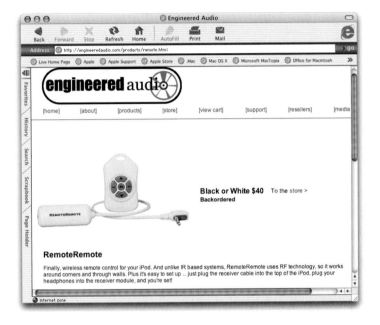

Earlier in this chapter I mentioned an RF wireless remote control that a friend bought me for my iPod. It's called RemoteRemote from Engineered Audio, and I absolutely love it for two reasons: (1) It's super small and super light—I've held feathers that weigh more—and the controller (they call it a "keyfob") is so small it can hang from your keychain if you like; and (2) it's RF (Radio Frequency) rather than IR. (What that means is that most remotes are "line-of-sight" infrared devices, which will work only if the iPod is clearly visible so that the beam from the remote can find the sensor on the iPod. However, with an RF remote like this one, I can keep my iPod in my glove compartment, and even though my iPod is "out-of-sight" in my closed glove compartment, it still works.) The wireless RemoteRemote lets you change tracks (next/previous tracks), fast forward and rewind, pause and play, and turn your volume up/down all wirelessly. It runs about $40 and is worth every penny, because it keeps you from messing with your iPod while you drive, and that keeps your eyes and attention on the road. Go to engineeredaudio.com to get one pronto!

TEN Technology's naviPod Wireless Remote

Another option for wireless iPod control is TEN Technology's naviPod. It's IR (rather than RF), so you'd want to consider this one if your iPod will be in fairly clear view (so no putting it in your glove compartment, unless you plan on driving around with your glove compartment's door open). You might also want to use this wireless remote to control your iPod in your house or office, where the iPod would be connected to a stereo (where it would again be in plain view). Like the RemoteRemote, its round-shaped controller has buttons for next/previous song, fast forward/rewind, volume up/down, and play/pause. It sells for around $50, and you can find it at either Apple's online store, Apple's retail stores, or at drbott.com.

Faking an iPod in Your Car

This book's Tech Editor, Terry White, came up with this idea for people who can't come up with a good (or inexpensive) enough way to connect their iPod to their car stereo. His trick uses your car's CD player to "fake" an iPod. You start in iTunes by creating a huge playlist of all your four- and five-star rated songs (we'll say that comes to around 280 songs, and in Terry's case, it would mostly be Charlie Daniels Band songs, with the occasional Marshall Tucker Band song thrown in for good measure). Normally, you'd transfer this playlist to your iPod, turn on the Shuffle feature, and play a random mix of your favorite songs as you go cruisin' down the highway. But, of course, you're not using an iPod, and you can't fit 280 songs on a CD. However, in Terry's version you burn this huge playlist to CD anyway (it makes more sense if you keep reading). Click in the Track Number column header, and then click on the Shuffle button (it's the second button from the left) in the bottom left-hand corner of the iTunes window. Now click on the Burn Disc button. When the first CD is full, it will automatically eject. You insert another blank disc, and the next songs in your playlist will burn until that CD is full. Then it will eject, and you insert another blank CD, and so on, until you've burned your 280 random songs on about 16 audio CDs that you can use in your CD player while you're cruisin' down the highway. Hey, it's not an iPod, but it sounds the same, it has the same randomness (shuffle), and you're hearing your favorite iTunes songs in your car. It's not perfect, but it's not *that* crazy (the emphasis is on the word "that").

Chapter Six

Freeze-Frame
Using the iPod photo

So, does this chapter win the award for "Most Obvious Chapter Title" or what? It's almost "too perfect" a name for a chapter on the iPod photo. (By the way, have you noticed that the "p" in the word "photo" is lowercase? Apple did it that way on purpose. Actually, I heard that when they first introduced it, it was named the "iPod Photo," but then Apple officially changed the "Photo" to the lowercase "photo" about a week or so later. Sources say it's so the iPod photo's naming convention will be consistent with other iPod products, like the iPod mini, which has a lowercase "m" on the "mini.") Now, why does all this matter? It matters plenty because although the book's editors and proofreaders don't read the actual introductions to books anymore, they do read these chapter intros. These people are really picky and insist on seeing things in these chapter intros like "long words" and punctuation. They also like it if I can work in a word or two of French, because then they get to use Microsoft Word's French dictionary, and apparently they get some kind of kickback or bonus. Plus they love to mention it casually in front of other editors: "I was working on Scott's book today, and I would have been done sooner, but I had to keep loading the French dictionary." The other editors all look at each other and go, "Ohhhhh. French!" So basically, I do it for them. They have so little—so a long word here (like existentialism) and a French phrase there (like "Mon oreille est une bouton de porte"), and they'll let lots of stuff slip by. Like this intro, for example.

Mac: Importing Photos into Your iPod photo

If you're a Mac user, the easiest way to get your photos from your Mac into your iPod photo is to use Apple's iPhoto application. Chances are that you're already using iPhoto for storing your images and, if so, you can just plug your iPod photo into your computer, then go directly to iTunes (I know, it seems like you'd go to iPhoto, but you don't—you go to iTunes). From the iTunes menu, choose Preferences, then click on the iPod icon and then click on the Photos tab. In the options listed, where it says Synchronize Photos From, choose iPhoto from the pop-up menu. Just below that menu, you can choose whether you want to import every single photo you have in iPhoto or just specific albums. If you choose the Copy All Photos and Albums route, you can take a lunch break because it could easily take an hour or more to import all your photos. Luckily, you only have to do this once. From then on, it'll just import any new photos you add to (or delete any photos you remove from) iPhoto.

Windows PC: Importing Photos into Your iPod photo

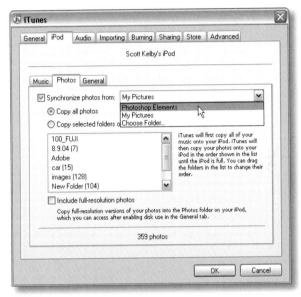

If you're using a PC, the easiest way to get your photos onto your iPod is to use Photoshop Album from Adobe (or Photoshop Elements 3, which has a version of Photoshop Album built right in, or you can use your My Pictures folder [see next page]). Photoshop Elements only costs about $99 and does a great job of sorting and managing all your photos (it's about the best Windows consumer-level photo-cataloging program out there). Just connect your iPod to your computer, then launch Apple's iTunes for Windows (it seems like you'd go to Photoshop Album or Elements 3, but you don't—you go to iTunes). From the Edit menu in iTunes, choose Preferences and then click on the iPod tab. When the dialog appears, click on the Photos tab, and then in the Synchronize Photos From pop-up menu, choose Photoshop Elements (or Photoshop Album if you're using that, or simply choose your My Pictures folder). Just below that menu, you can choose whether you want to import every single photo you have (in an album) or just specific images (or albums). If you choose the Copy All Photos route, you can take a lunch break because it could easily take an hour or more to import all your photos. Luckily, you only have to do this once. From then on, it'll just import any new photos you add or delete any photos you remove.

Importing Just Specific Photo Albums

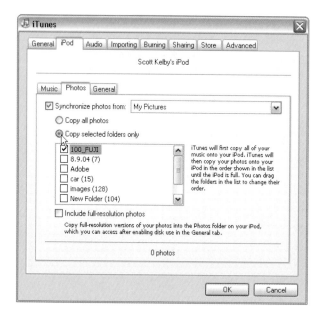

By default, when you connect your iPod photo to your computer, it wants to import every single photo you have in your iPhoto library (or on your PC, your Photoshop Album or Photoshop Elements collection, or individual folders within your My Pictures folder). This can take, well...it seems like forever, but it's probably only an hour or so. You can speed up this process by importing only the specific albums you want imported. That way, only your favorite photos are copied onto your iPod photo, and not *every* photo you have. To do this, connect your iPod photo to your computer, launch iTunes, then click on the iPod Options button in the bottom right-hand corner of the iTunes window. When the iPod dialog appears, click on the Photos tab, then click on the button labeled Copy Selected Folders (Albums) Only. In the area below, click the checkbox beside each album you want imported. When you click OK, only those albums will be imported, saving you lots of time (and space on your iPod photo).

---

iTip

You don't have to use Photoshop Album or Photoshop Elements to create separate collections of your photos. Just create separate folders inside your My Pictures folder. Name each folder with the name you want for a collection, and then drag the photos you want to appear in each collection into the corresponding folder. Then when you import photos from your My Pictures folder, any folders inside the My Pictures folder will import as separate collections that you can access from the Photos menu on your iPod photo.

Viewing Photos You've Imported

Once you've copied your photos over onto your iPod photo, viewing them is easy. From the Main Menu, just use the Click Wheel to scroll down to Photos, then press the Select button. Any imported albums will appear here. To see the photos in a particular album, use the Click Wheel to scroll to that album, then press the Select button again. In just a moment, tiny thumbnails of the photos in your selected album will appear. The selected thumbnail will have a yellow highlight around it. To see that photo, just press the Select button again and the photo will fill your screen. To see the next photo, press the Fast Forward button. To see the previous photo, press the Previous/Rewind button. To scroll quickly through your images at full-screen size, just glide around the Click Wheel clockwise (to move quickly forward) or counter-clockwise (to move quickly back to the beginning of that album).

Seeing Full-Color Album Art

One of my favorite features of the iPod photo is that it can display the full-color album art for the currently playing song (provided you either found album art for it when the song was first in iTunes, or you downloaded the song from the iTunes Music Store, where the album art is automatically included). By default, if you have album art, a small thumbnail of it is displayed to the left of the currently playing song, but if you'd like to see a full-screen version of that album art, just press the center Select button. To return to the standard view, press the center Select button once again.

Seeing a Slideshow

To see a slideshow of your photos, just go to the photo album you want to see, then press on the center Select button to select any image thumbnail, which will switch to full-screen, then press the Select button again to start your slideshow in full-screen. To stop your slideshow and return to the thumbnail view, press the Menu button. To pause a running slideshow, press the Play/Pause button. To restart it, just press Play/Pause again.

Adding Music to Your Slideshow

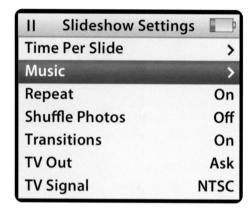

If there's one thing a slideshow definitely needs, it's a music track playing behind it. You can add music in one of two ways—you can assign a song in iPhoto, then you can have it play automatically when you choose a particular album (collection) for your slideshow, or you can choose one from right within your iPod photo. To assign a song in iPhoto, go to iPhoto, click on the album you want, then click on the Slideshow button near the bottom-left corner of iPhoto. When the Slideshow dialog appears, click on the Music button, then choose which song you'd like to have playing behind this album (you can choose any song from your iTunes Library). Then, plug in your iPod photo and let it update. Now, from the iPod photo's Main Menu, choose Photos, choose Slideshow Settings, choose Music, then scroll all the way to the top and choose From iPhoto. Now when you play your slideshow, it will use the music you chose in iPhoto. If you'd prefer to choose your background music "on the fly," then go to the iPod photo's Main Menu, choose Photos, choose Slideshow Settings, choose Music, then choose which playlist you'd like to play during the slideshow. Now you can press Play/Pause.

---

iTip

Even though in iPhoto you can pick either a single song or a playlist, in iPod photo you can only pick a playlist. The only way to get a single song in iPod photo is to select a playlist that only has one song in it.

Changing the Duration of Each Slide

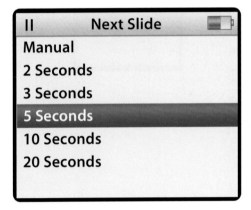

By default, each slide will remain on your iPod photo screen for 3 seconds. If you'd like it to remain onscreen longer (or shorter for that matter), just go to the Main Menu, choose Photos, choose Slideshow Settings, then select Time Per Slide and choose from the list of times. *Note:* Manual means you'll click the Fast Forward button on the Click Wheel to move to the next slide. So what's the difference between this and just displaying a regular photo, then pressing Fast Forward to see the next photo? One thing—the slideshow has a smooth "wipe" transition between photos, whereas just pressing Fast Forward when a photo is displayed gives you a harsh, immediate "cut" to the next photo.

Using Your iPod photo for Presentations

Want to really "tune up" the crowd at your next business presentation? Instead of lugging your laptop to the conference room and hooking up to a projector, just bring along your iPod photo and the AV cable that came with it, and you can just connect your iPod directly to the projector. Instead of showing photos, show a slide presentation of your album and use the iPod's Fast Forward button to advance to the next slide. Of course, you can even have music behind your slide presentation. If you really want to take things up a notch, get the naviPod Wireless IR Remote, so you can stand in the front of the room and control your iPod photo (advancing it through your presentation slides) while it sits quietly back there by the projector.

iTip

While in Slideshow mode, you can see your next photo on the iPod photo screen before everyone else. This is cool for doing presentations and knowing which photo or slide is coming up next.

Seeing Your Slideshow on TV

To see your slideshow on TV, use the AV cable that came with your iPod photo to connect it to the inputs on your TV. Put the thin, single jack into the AV output on the top
of your iPod photo, then insert the red, yellow, and white audio and video connectors
into the input jacks on your TV. (*Note:* If you're a freak for high-quality image display,
you can use the S-video connector to connect to your TV instead. To use S-video, you'll
have to place your iPod photo into its Dock [that came with it], then attach an S-video
cable [you'll have to buy one—it's not included] to the S-video output on the back
of the Dock, and connect the other end to your TV's S-video input.) Once connected,
scroll to the photo album you want to display as a slideshow, but instead of pressing
the center Select button, press the Play/Pause button. This brings up a dialog window,
and at the bottom you can scroll down to TV On, which sets your iPod photo to display
on a TV. Now press the center Select button to begin your "big screen" experience.
(*Note:* If you connect your iPod photo Dock via the S-video cable, you also need to connect the line out to your TV or stereo speakers via an audio cable, also not included. The
included TV cables *only* work from the headphone jack on top of the iPod.)

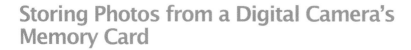
Storing Photos from a Digital Camera's Memory Card

If you're shooting with a digital camera, you can back up (or completely move) your digital photos directly from your camera's memory card right onto the iPod (no computer required) using Belkin's Media Reader for iPod (which works on any iPod except the mini). This $99 accessory lets you insert your digital camera's memory card into the reader, which connects and downloads the photos into a folder on your iPod. This is great for when you're shooting on location (or on vacation) and want to copy your digital camera photos (for safekeeping). *Note:* Remember, you're just "storing and transporting" these memory-card photos—you won't be able to view them on your iPod photo. *Another Note:* As of this writing, the Belkin Media Reader for iPod supports most major digital camera memory cards, including CompactFlash (Type 1 and 2), Smart-Media, Secure Digital (SD), Memory Stick, and MultiMedia Card (MMC). *Final Note:* The photos will be imported automatically into iPhoto upon your next sync.

Deleting Rolls of Photos from Your iPod

If you decide that you'd like to delete a roll of photos you've imported from your digital camera's card reader, start at the Main Menu and choose Photos. Then scroll down using the Click Wheel and choose Photo Import, and in the menu that appears you'll see a list of rolls you've imported. To delete a roll, just scroll down to highlight the roll you want and press the center Select button. The next screen that appears will give you the information for the currently selected roll, and Delete Roll will be highlighted (by default). To delete the roll, press the center Select button again. If you choose Delete Roll, it does give you one last chance (since deleting is a permanent thing, it wants to be sure that's really what you want to do). If you're sure you want to delete, scroll down to Delete and press the center Select button. That's it—that roll of stored photos from your digital camera's memory card will be deleted from your iPod.

Getting Your Stored Photos Back on Your Computer

You've backed up a bunch of photos onto your iPod, and now you want to get them back into your computer so you can edit them, sort them, and, if you like, transfer them from your computer back to your iPod. Here's how to do just that: Connect your iPod to your computer, then go to iTunes. When you launch iTunes, you'll see your iPod listed in the Source list on the left side of the iTunes window. Click on your iPod and an iPod Options button will appear in the lower right-hand corner of the iTunes window. Click on this button to make the iPod Options visible, then click on the General tab, and turn on the checkbox for Enable Disk Use. Once you do this, the iPod will appear on your computer as a mounted disk (like a hard disk or USB device). Go to your computer's desktop, double-click on the now-visible iPod, and you'll see a DCIM folder with your imported photos (don't disturb the folder named Photos). Now you can select these photos and drag them onto your computer.

---

iTip

You can also import photos using software such as iPhoto (Mac), or Photoshop Elements or Photoshop Album (Windows). To do that, put the iPod into its Dock, then (on a Mac) go to iPhoto, click the Import button, navigate to a folder on your iPod photo named DCIM, and import those photos. If you're using Windows, connect the iPod to your computer, launch Photoshop Elements 3 (or Photoshop Album), then go under the File menu in the Organizer, under Get Photos, and navigate your way to the iPod. Then on the iPod, locate the folder named DCIM and "Get" those photos.

Getting Info on Your Imported Digital Camera Photos

If you're using the iPod to back up photos from your digital camera using a card reader (as previously mentioned), you can find out some additional information (like when each roll was imported, the number of photos, the format, etc.) by going under the Main Menu and choosing Photos, then under the Photos menu choosing Import Photos (you'll only see this menu when you have a memory card reader attached to your iPod). Then under the Import Photos menu choose the roll number you'd like info on, and the info for that roll will appear in the display.

---

iTip

If you're using your iPod to store files or backups, having iTunes launch each time you connect your iPod photo can be incredibly irritating. What's worse is if you're connecting your iPod photo as a hard drive to another computer, iTunes will automatically sync with that computer. Luckily, you can turn off this "auto iTunes launch" by connecting your iPod to your computer, then clicking on the iPod Options button in the bottom right-hand corner of the iTunes window. When the iPod dialog appears, click on the General tab, then uncheck the Open iTunes When This iPod is Attached option and click OK. That's it—no more auto-launch.

Chapter Seven

Home Sweet Home

iTunes Essentials

Now, I know what you're thinking: "How does Motley Crue's 'Home Sweet Home' tie into a chapter about the basic, most essential things you need to know about iTunes?" First, many of you will be using iTunes at home (unless of course, you're like my employees, who use iTunes all day long in lieu of working productively. In fact, when I'm roaming the halls, I'm not sure which I see more on their monitors—iTunes, eBay, Amazon.com, or CNN. Once I saw someone with Photoshop open, but thankfully it was just because they were color-correcting an album cover they were going to use in iTunes. Whew—that was a close one!). Anyway, since some of you will be using iTunes at home, especially when you first get your iPod, I thought there was some loose thread I could use to connect your using your iPod there with the word "home" in "Home Sweet Home." Hey, it's fairly "loose" I know, but my backup plan was to use the song "Essential" by The Gravy, from their album *Lollipolyp*. I didn't have a problem with the "polyp" part of it (as icky as that is), but if the chapter title was "Essential" and the subtitle was "iTunes Essentials," you'd think I took the easy way out, and you deserve more than that. You deserve a title that is so loosely related to the actual topic of the chapter that it takes more than 300 words to explain why I chose it. See, just when you think you've got me figured out, I zig when you thought I'd zag (I have no idea what that means). Quick, turn the page before I think of something else to write here.

Limiting How Much iTunes Displays

In the iTunes main window (where you see your songs), there are separate columns that display the song title, the artist, the album name, and a host of other information. Some of it you probably will care about (like the song name, artist, time, etc.), and some of it you probably won't need to see. Ever. Stuff like a song's beats per minute (although this column is helpful to DJs). Luckily, you can customize your columns and choose which ones are visible, which makes for very clean, easy-to-read playlists, because they display just the info you care about seeing. Here's how to customize yours: Press Command-J (PC: Control-J) on your keyboard to bring up the iTunes View Options dialog. Select which columns you'd like to be visible by turning on (or off) the checkboxes next to the column names. When you're done, click OK and only the checked columns will appear in your main window.

---

iTip

If at any time you decide you want a hidden column to be visible, just Control–click (PC: Right–click) directly on one of the column headers. This brings up a contextual menu of column choices. Just choose the column you want to see (hidden ones will be the ones without a checkmark), and that column will now be visible. To hide any column, you do the same trick, but uncheck the column you wish to hide.

Getting More Song Info

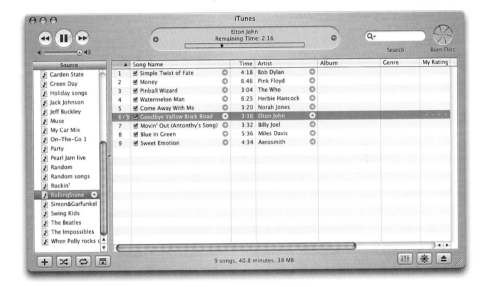

iTunes' status display (that pill-shaped panel at the top center of the iTunes window) shows you the name of the current song, the artist, and how much of the song has already played (in minutes and seconds), which is called the elapsed time. If you'd like the name of the album the song came from, click directly on the artist's name (or the song name, depending on which is visible when you go to click). If instead of elapsed time, you'd like to know how much time is left until the song has finished playing (the remaining time), click directly on the words "Elapsed Time" in the status display, and the Remaining Time will appear. Want the total time of the song? Click in the same place.

---

iTip

To the left of each song title is a checkbox, and every checked song will play when playing an entire playlist. If you want to skip a song, just uncheck its checkbox. This also works when importing songs from an audio CD—checked songs are imported, unchecked songs are not.

Editing Your Song's Info

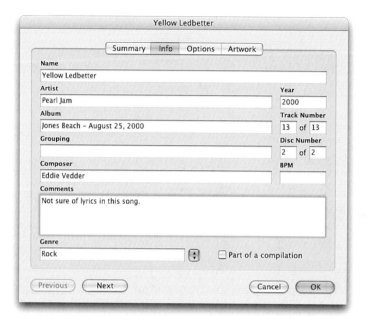

If you want to change, update, or add any information to a song, just Control-click (PC: Right-click) on the song, and from the contextual menu that appears, choose Get Info. When the dialog appears, click on the Info tab and you'll see a number of fields where you can edit or add information about the song. This is the same information that will appear in the status display (in the top center of the iTunes window) when a song is playing, but you can also include additional information, like the year it was recorded, your own personal comments, and the song's composer. When you're done, just click the OK button.

---

iTip

There are really four different ways to play a song within iTunes, so you should try them all to find out which one best suits your personal style. Here they are: (1) Find the song you want to play and just double-click on it; (2) click on the song you want to play and then press the Spacebar on your keyboard; (3) click on the song you want to hear, then click on the Play button in the upper left-hand corner of the iTunes window; or (4) click on the song you want to play and choose Play from the Controls menu.

Editing More Than One Song at One Time

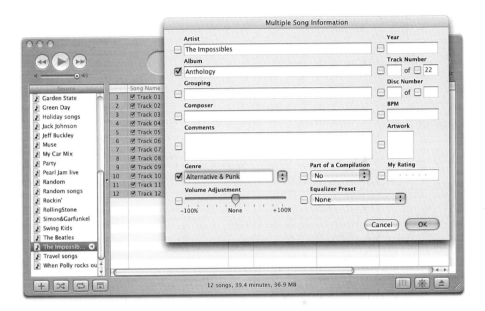

You know by now how to edit a song's info (using the Get Info dialog), but what if you want to edit a bunch of songs at once (for example, let's say you imported 12 songs from an album, and you want to add the album name to each of the 12 songs)? You do that by Command-clicking (PC: Control-clicking) on the songs you want to edit (in this case, all 12 songs you just imported), and then Control-clicking (PC: Right-clicking) on any one of those 12 songs. Rather than the standard Get Info dialog, a Multiple Song Information dialog will appear instead (well, the first time you do this, you'll get a warning dialog that says something like: "Are you sure you want to edit the information for multiple songs?" Just click OK). Now the information you enter in this dialog will be applied to all the selected songs. When you're done, just click OK.

Updating Just One Info Field

If you want to change just one bit of info on a song (for example, let's say you had the song "Hate to Say I Told You So" by The Hives listed as coming from their album *Barely Legal* when anyone who's anyone knows that song actually came from the album *Veni Vidi Vicious*), here's good news: You don't have to bring up the whole Get Info dialog for just this one little change. Instead, just click on the song, and then click once directly on the album's current name to highlight the Album field. Now, just type in the new name over the old name, then press the Enter key to lock in your change. It probably goes without saying, but I'm going to say it anyway—this also works for editing other fields, like Song Name, Artist, etc.

Changing the Sort Order: Last to First

By default, iTunes columns are sorted in either alphabetical order or numerically (from the lowest number to the highest). You can determine how iTunes is sorting by looking for the column that has the little arrow on the right side. If the arrow is facing upward, the column is sorted from A to Z (alphabetically) or from lowest number to highest (numerically). However, if you'd prefer to have it sort backwards (so you'd hear U2's "Vertigo" before you'd hear "My Happy Ending" by Avril Lavigne), just click once on the Artist column header. This reverses the alphabetical order (you'll now see the little arrow in the Artist column pointing downward), putting "Vertigo" at the top of the playlist (or if you click on a numerical column, like Time, then your longest song would be first, followed by your next longest, etc., until your shortest song appeared at the bottom). Also, if you click on the My Rating column, your 5-star songs will appear at the top of the iTunes window, and if you click again, they'll appear at the bottom of the iTunes window.

Finding the Song That's Playing Now

When you click on a song, that song highlights so you know it's selected. When you click the Play button, a tiny speaker icon appears to the right of the track number—that speaker icon (not the highlighting) indicates which song is playing. Often you'll wind up playing a song, and while that song is playing in the background, you'll go on to do other things. You might be sorting another playlist, changing song names, etc. So, although you may be playing the song "All Eyes Upon You" by Figdish, that song won't be highlighted because you're working in an entirely different playlist. Then, how do you find the song that's currently playing? Just press Command-L (PC: Control-L), which instantly jumps you to the song that's currently playing, even if it's in a different playlist.

---

iTip

If you can't get enough of a particular song (or a particular playlist for that matter), you can have iTunes automatically repeat it by clicking on the Repeat Playlist/Song button (it's the third button from the left in the bottom-left corner of the iTunes window). If you click once on this button, iTunes will repeat your entire current playlist. Click again and it will replay the current song over and over and over again (toddlers love this feature). To stop the repeating, click the button again.

Finding a Song

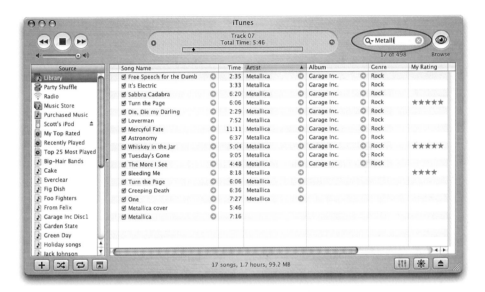

Once you have a couple hundred (or more) songs in your Library, you'll be amazed at how hard it is to track down a particular song. That's why iTunes has a Search field in the upper right-hand corner of the iTunes window (it's the field with the Magnifying Glass icon in it). While in the Library, just begin typing the name of the song, album, or artist, and as you start typing, iTunes will immediately start searching. As soon as it finds a match (even if you haven't finished typing), it'll display the matches in the main window. To clear the search results and return to your previous playlist, just click on the little gray circle with an "X" in it (on the right side of the Search field).

---

iTip

By default, when you use the Search function, iTunes searches everything: song names, artists, composers, etc. If you want to speed things up, you can narrow your search to just song name, album name, etc., by clicking on the Magnifying Glass icon. A pop-up menu will appear in which you can choose what criteria you want to search.

Finding Songs by Browsing

This happened to me the other day: My 8-year-old son and I were driving to the mall (well, I was driving), and we were listening to our iPod on the way. My son pleaded to hear some Bon Jovi, so I browsed on my iPod and within seconds we were listening to "Bad Medicine," followed by "Livin' on a Prayer" on our "temporary" playlist. Well, there's a Browse feature in iTunes that lets you create your own "temporary" playlist. In the mood for country music but don't have a "country" playlist? Use Browse. Here's how: Go to the Library (Browse only works when you're in the Library), then click the Browse button in the upper-right corner of the iTunes window. This gives you three main categories to browse through: Genre, Artist, and Album. In the Genre list click on Country and all your Country songs will instantly appear (well, at least all the songs you tagged with the Country genre). Just double-click the first song in the list that appears and you're set. In the Bon Jovi case, I would've just clicked on Bon Jovi in the Artist section instead.

---

iTip

Some people just don't like taking the time to add genres to all their songs, so if you're not a "genre" person, you may as well hide the Genre category when you're browsing. Just go to iTunes Preferences (on the Mac, it's under the iTunes menu; on a Windows PC, it's under the Edit menu) and click on the General tab. Then turn off the checkbox for Show Genre When Browsing.

Adding Your Own Custom Genres

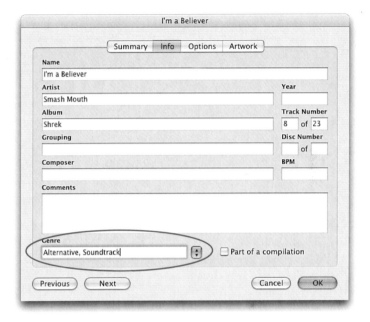

Although iTunes comes with a preset list of popular genres, there are some it just doesn't include (like Salsa, Thrash, or New Wave), and you can probably come up with a dozen or so yourself. That's why iTunes lets you create your own custom genres (like Death Metal or Industrial). To create a custom genre, Control-click (PC: Right-click) on any song, and then choose Get Info from the contextual menu that appears. When the Get Info dialog appears, click on the Info tab, and then just type the name you want for your "new" genre in the Genre field (how about Broadway Musicals or Gospel?) and click OK. If you want to create a genre that encompasses a number of different styles, just put a comma after each name (like Metal, Jazz, Punk, Choral). Assigning these "multiple genres" to a song will cause the song to appear in multiple categories when searching or browsing. For example, you might want certain Smash Mouth songs to have multiple genres, so they appear both in Alternative and Soundtracks (a lot of Smash Mouth songs end up on soundtracks for movies, like *Shrek*).

Clearing a Song's Play Count

As you know by now, iTunes keeps a count of each time you play a particular song, but if at any time you'd like to wipe that play count clean (for example, if you're having friends over and you don't want them to see that you've played "Wake Me Up Before You Go-Go" by Wham! 87 times), just Control-click (PC: Right-click) on the song and from the contextual menu that appears, choose Reset Play Count. iTunes will reset your play count to zero. Your secret will now be safe forever, and your friends will think you're cool once again. (*Note:* Although you've cleared the Play Count field, the Last Played field will still show—obviously—the last time you played the song, so there's still something that might give your secret away....)

Deleting Songs

If you've had enough of a song and you just want it out of iTunes (and out of your life), just click on the song and press the Delete (PC: Backspace) key on your keyboard. You can also delete a song by Control-clicking (PC: Right-clicking) on a song and choosing Clear from the contextual menu that appears. If the song is in a playlist, iTunes will remove the song from just that playlist. If you click on a song in your main Library, then iTunes removes the file altogether and puts it in the Trash (on a Mac) or the Recycling Bin (on a PC). Don't freak out—you'll get a warning dialog before it does either, so you don't have to worry about hitting the wrong key and losing a beloved treasured favorite, like "Disposable Teens" by Marilyn Manson.

---

iTip

To delete multiple songs at once, just Command–click (PC: Control–click) on all the songs you want to delete, then press the Delete (PC: Backspace) key on your keyboard. If you want to select a whole group of contiguous songs, just click on the first song in the group you want to delete, then hold the Shift key, scroll down to the last song, and click on it. All the songs between where you clicked will be highlighted. To delete them all with one keystroke, just press the Delete (PC: Backspace) key. (Note: Remember, if you're deleting from your iTunes Library, this is a permanent action; if you're deleting within a playlist, the song remains in your Library.)

iTunes' Built-In VU Meters

If you ever need to see a graphic display of the audio frequencies in your song (it's helpful when you're recording so you don't record at too high a volume, which causes distortion), go up to the status display (in the top center of the iTunes window) and on the far-left side of the display, click on the dark gray circular button with a right-facing arrow. When you do this, two digital VU (volume unit) meters will appear where the song info usually appears, giving you a visualization of the music frequencies (just in case you care).

Organizing the Songs on Your Hard Disk

If you have an MP3 song on your hard disk and you double-click on it, iTunes opens it and plays the song. It also creates an invisible shortcut (or alias) to that song from that folder on your hard disk. There's nothing wrong with this, but what you'll eventually have are folders scattered all over your hard disk with music in them. Well, you can make things much more organized than that (which makes backing up your music much easier) by having iTunes copy each song that it plays into the iTunes Music folder. That way, all of your music is in one place. To turn on this feature, go to the iTunes Preferences (on a Mac, it's under the iTunes menu; on a Windows PC, it's under the Edit menu), and when the Preferences dialog appears, click on the Advanced tab. In the Advanced section turn on the checkbox for Copy Files to iTunes Music Folder When Adding to Library. Now you can click OK, with the peace of mind that can only come from bringing order and harmony to your music world.

---

iTip

If you've already got music scattered all over your hard disk, it's not too late—you can have iTunes go to all those folders and copy all the songs listed in your Library into the iTunes Music folder on your hard disk in just one click. Go under the Advanced menu and choose Consolidate Library. It wouldn't hurt if you played the song "Come Together" by The Beatles while you're doing this.

from CD to Playlist

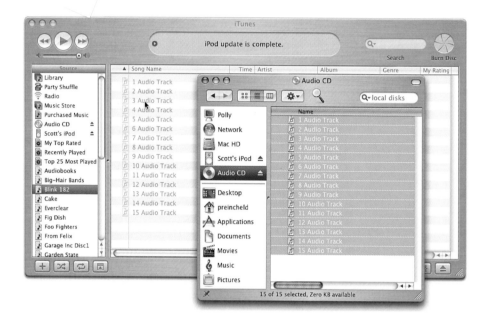

When you import songs from a CD, it usually works like this: You import the songs; you find them in your iTunes Library; and then you drag these imported songs into a playlist. Want to skip a step? Then when you import a CD, select the songs on the CD (by Shift-clicking on the first and last song in the CD's folder on your hard disk), and drag them right into that new playlist. When they import, of course, they'll be in your Library, but they'll also be in your desired playlist. Hey, if it saves time, I'm all for it.

iTip

If you have MP3 songs already on your hard disk that you want to add to your iTunes Library, it's easy: Just go under the File menu and choose Add to Library. This brings up a standard Open dialog, so you can navigate to where the songs are on your hard disk, then click the Choose button to add them. Of course, there's an even easier way—just open the folder that has your MP3 songs, drag-and-drop them right into iTunes, and they'll be imported. It doesn't get much easier than that.

Setting Up Your CDs to Import Automatically

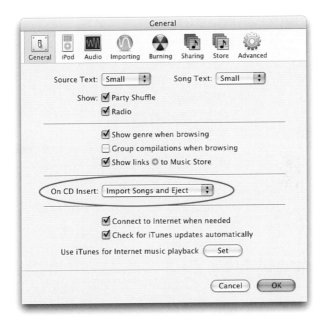

If you've decided to import your entire collection of CDs into iTunes (and I whole-heartedly recommend that), then you're going to want to have as much automation as possible, so you don't go totally brain-dead during the process. Here's why: When you insert a CD, it doesn't import the tracks. Instead, it just shows you what's on the CD, which is great if you only want to hear what's on the CD. But if you're cataloguing your entire collection, this is the last thing you want it to do. Instead, imagine how much time it would save if you just inserted a CD and iTunes automatically imported all the songs, then spit the CD out, ready for you to insert the next disc? It can do just that—you just have to tell it to. Go to iTunes Preferences (found under the iTunes menu on a Mac; the Edit menu on a Windows PC), and then click on the General tab. From the On CD Insert pop-up menu, choose Import Songs and Eject, and then click OK. That's it—you just turned your computer into an automatic CD-importing machine, which enables you to pay your little brother to sit there and swap the ejected CDs for a few hours while you go to a concert. See, this is what life's all about.

Auto-Naming for Imported CD Songs

If you're importing songs from a CD, and you're connected to the Internet, you may be able to save yourself loads of time by having iTunes automatically find the names (and other background info) for all the songs you're importing. Here's what actually happens: When you turn on this option, iTunes will go to the Web and search within the massive Gracenote CDDB Internet Audio Database for the info on the CD you're importing. If it finds the information, iTunes will automatically download that information into each song's info panel, naming the songs (artists, album names, etc.) as it goes (pretty cool, eh?). To turn on this way-cool feature, go to iTunes Preferences (under the iTunes menu on a Mac; the Edit menu on a Windows PC), and then click on the General tab. Now turn on the checkbox for Connect to Internet When Needed. That's it—when you start importing a CD, iTunes will go to that website, find the info, and enter all the names (and background info) for you automatically.

Saving Hard Disk Space When Importing CDs

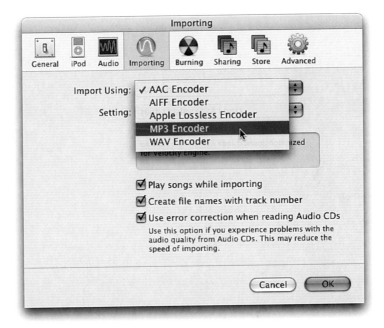

When you import music from CDs, by default iTunes converts your songs into AAC format (which is great in that it compresses the size of your song files while maintaining CD-quality sound). But if you need to import smaller-sized files (and you don't mind a decrease in sound quality), you can choose to import songs as MP3s. Just go into iTunes Preferences (under the iTunes menu on a Mac; the Edit menu on a Windows PC), and then click on the Importing tab. From the Import Using pop-up menu, choose MP3 Encoder (or any other file format you'd like). Now when you import CD songs, they'll be in the format you want. (By the way, all songs from the iTunes Music Store are protected AAC encoded, meaning the file can't be "shared," while most CD-imported files are unprotected AAC encoded, meaning the files can be shared.)

Combining Two Tracks into One

Sometimes when you import a song from a CD, if the song has a lengthy introduction, it can get separated from the song. For example, look at Van Halen's classic cover of "You Really Got Me." It starts with a legendary guitar solo from Eddie Van Halen that actually has its own name ("Eruption"), but if you hear this song on classic rock radio stations, the two are played as one song, as "Eruption" goes right into "You Really Got Me." It's really one song, but when you import it from the CD, there's a decent chance iTunes will import it as two separate songs (so there will be a gap of a few seconds between songs). If that happens, no sweat—just Command-click (PC: Control-click) on the two songs before they're imported and then go under the Advanced menu and choose Join CD Tracks. Now, they'll import as one song, with no gap in between (you'll know that they're linked because a tiny bracket icon will appear next to the top song's name). By the way, if you ever want to really mess with rock history, you can select both songs, go under the Advanced menu, and choose Unjoin CD Tracks. (*Note:* This whole joining thing can only happen *before* the CD tracks are imported into iTunes—not after.)

Salvaging Damaged CDs

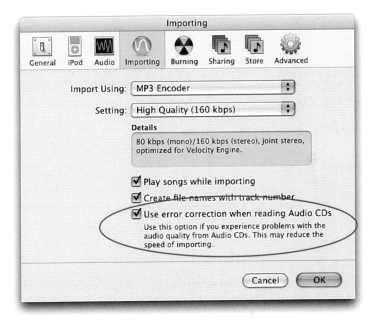

If you find out that your little sister has been using one of your prized CDs as a Frisbee, you're probably going to find that out when you play the CD in iTunes. It's going to have its share of scratches, junk, and other nasty stuff, which makes importing these tracks nearly out of the question—unless you know about this somewhat weird and obscure preference setting. To find it, go into iTunes Preferences (found under the iTunes menu on a Mac; the Edit menu on a Windows PC), and then click on the Importing tab. Now turn on the checkbox for Use Error Correction When Reading Audio CDs. iTunes will then do its darnedest to correct a disc's trauma while importing, salvaging as much as it can. It doesn't work 100% of the time, but when it does, it's worth its weight in Starbucks coffee.

Burning a CD

Burning a CD is a breeze, but there are a couple of things you should know before you do it, just so it's even breezier (if that's even a word). First, you can only burn playlists (not your Library), so click on a playlist in the Source list that you want to burn (also, don't insert a blank CD yet—wait until it asks you to). So now that you've selected a playlist, take a quick look down at the bottom center of the iTunes window to make sure you don't have more than 1.2 hours of music in your playlist (that's pretty much the amount of time you can fit onto an audio CD these days). If you have too many songs, delete some songs until you have less than 1.2 hours. Then click on the Burn Disc button (it's in the upper right-hand corner of the iTunes window). The top-center status display will prompt you: Please Insert a Blank Disc (that's your cue). Once you insert a blank CD, iTunes will prompt you to Click Burn Disc to Start. (*Note:* Now's your chance to abort burning the CD, if you so desire, by clicking on the "X" in the status display.) Now iTunes will begin to burn the songs in your playlist onto your blank CD. Assuming all goes well, iTunes will spit your new music CD out of your CD drive.

---

iTip

If there's a song in your playlist that you don't want to appear on a CD that you're getting ready to burn, just click on the checkbox that appears right before the song's name to deselect it, and when the CD burns, iTunes will skip over the unchecked song.

Fitting More Songs on Your CDs

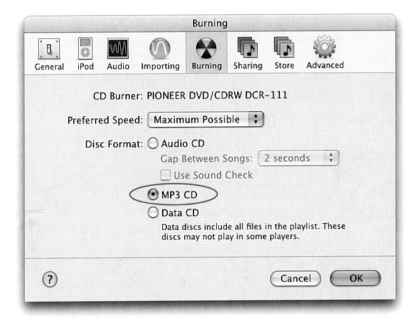

If you want to fit the maximum number of songs on your CDs, you might want to try burning an MP3 CD rather than an audio CD (provided of course that your CD player can read MP3 CDs—many new CD players can, but not all). Because the MP3 format uses a high rate of compression, you'll be able to fit many more songs on a CD in MP3 format, but to do that, you'll need to change an iTunes Preference setting. So, go to iTunes Preferences (found under the iTunes menu on a Mac; the Edit menu on a Windows PC), and then click on the Burning tab. Under the Disc Format section, click on MP3 CD, and then click OK. That's all there is to it—now you just have to hope that your CD player supports MP3 CDs. (*Note:* This doesn't work for iTunes Music Store songs or songs in AAC format.)

Setting the Gap between Burned Songs

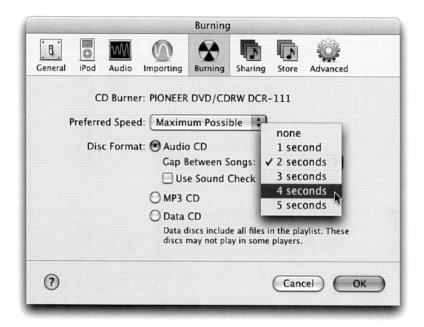

So your CDs don't sound like one long, unending song, iTunes adds a 2-second pause (or gap) between songs by default. Besides being sorely needed from a listening perspective, the gap also helps your CD player recognize individual tracks. Although 2 seconds is the default setting, you can change the length of the gap so it's longer, shorter, or you can eliminate the gap altogether (which you might want to do if you're listening to an audiobook or the recording of a speech). To do that, go to iTunes Preferences (found under the iTunes menu on a Mac; the Edit menu on a Windows PC), and then click on the Burning tab. Choose your desired length (in seconds) from the Gap Between Songs pop-up menu, and then click OK. That length now becomes the gap setting for your burned CDs.

Chapter Eight

Imaginary Player

Playlists and Smart Playlists

▶▶ Hey, it's not easy finding a song with the word "playlist" in it. Or a movie. Or a TV show. So, after doing some searching, I got as close as I was going to get with the song "Imaginary Player" by Jay-Z. Now, in the iTunes Music Store, there are two different versions of this song—one with the Explicit lyrics warning and one with the Clean label. Normally, I just go with the Clean version, because I'm a wholesome, family man myself. (However, one time I actually got "burned" when downloading the Clean version of a song. It was the song "1985" by Bowling for Soup. My wife heard the song on Radio Disney, told me about it, and when I found it on the iTunes Music Store, it had both Explicit and Clean versions, so of course I downloaded the Clean version for my son's playlist on my iPod. However, Apple's definition of Clean is obviously different than Radio Disney's. For example, on the Radio Disney version of the song, the second verse goes: "She was gonna be an actress. She was gonna be a star. She was gonna shake it, on the hood of Whitesnake's car." The "shake it" part's a little suggestive, but it's certainly not explicit. However, in the Clean version I downloaded, instead it says: "She was gonna shake her ass, on the hood of Whitesnake's car." Unsuspecting, I played it in front of my son, only once mind you, but of course he's memorized that line verbatim. Kids!) Anyway, this chapter isn't about the explicit version of either Jay-Z's or Bowling for Soup's song, but if it were, I'd probably sell a lot more books.

127

Creating Your Own Playlists

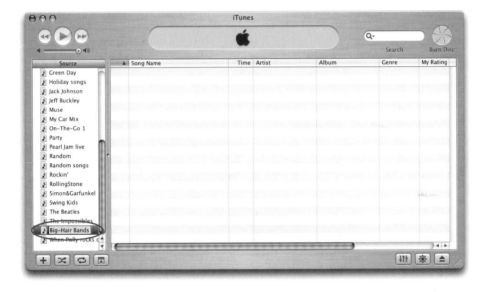

Playlists are like your own custom collections of songs (like you might have a playlist of mellow music, or driving music, or big-hair bands of the '80s, etc.). Creating playlists takes just two steps. The first is to click the Create a Playlist button at the bottom left-hand corner of the iTunes window. Your new playlist will appear in the Source list along the left of the iTunes window, and the name field for your playlist will already be highlighted so you can name it. Type in a name and press the Enter key to lock it in. Now, in the Source list, click on the Library icon so you can see all your songs in the iTunes window, then simply drag-and-drop songs from your Library onto your new playlist's icon. To see the songs in your playlist (or to play your playlist), just click on the playlist in the Source list.

Removing Songs from a Playlist

If a playlist includes a song that just plain shouldn't be there (for example, if "We Built This City" by Starship winds up on your Cool Songs playlist), you can remove it fast by clicking on it and pressing the Delete (PC: Backspace) key on your keyboard. Now, what if a song like "Muskrat Love" or Achy Breaky Heart" somehow wound up on that playlist as well? You can remove multiple bad songs by Command-clicking (PC: Control-clicking) on them and then pressing Delete (or you can Control-click [PC: Right-click] on any of those selected songs and choose Clear from the contextual menu that appears), instantly wiping their innate lameness from your playlist. (*Note:* This won't remove the songs from your iTunes Library; it will only remove them from the playlist.)

---

iTip

If you've got a song in one of your playlists that you don't want to delete, but you don't want to hear it right now, you can just temporarily skip over it by unchecking the check-box that appears directly before the song's name (only checked songs will be played when playing a playlist). If you later decide you want to hear that song in the playlist, just turn on the checkbox beside it.

Removing an Entire Playlist

If you've created a playlist, and you just don't want it anymore (let's say you created a Christmas playlist and now it's February), just Control-click (PC: Right-click) on the playlist in the Source list on the left-hand side of the iTunes window and choose Clear from the contextual menu. That's it—it's gone. Or even better: Just click on the playlist to select it in the Source list and press the Delete (PC: Backspace) key. *Note:* Only the playlist is gone—it doesn't remove the songs from your main iTunes Library.

Another Way to Create Playlists

Throughout this book, when we talk about creating a regular playlist, we generally talk about dragging-and-dropping songs from your Library into your playlist, but there's another quick way to create a custom playlist. Just Command-click (PC: Control-click) on all the songs in your Library that you want in your playlist, and then go under the File menu and choose New Playlist From Selection (or press Shift-Command-N [PC: Shift-Control-N]). All the selected songs will be gathered into a new playlist, and it will appear in the Source list with a name field already highlighted, so all you have to do is type in your new playlist's name and press Enter.

---

iTip

When you click on a playlist, that playlist appears in the main iTunes window, replacing whatever was visible before (like perhaps your Library). However, if you'd like a playlist to open in its own separate floating window (leaving your original window still open and untouched), instead of clicking on your playlist, just double-click on its icon in the Source list.

Making a List of Your Playlists

If you'd like a printed list of one (or more) of your playlists and their contents (hey, don't laugh—this is handy if your hard drive has a major crash and you haven't backed up in a while…or ever), iTunes can make one for you. First, in the Source list on the left side of the iTunes window, Control-click (PC: Right-click) on the playlist that you want to print and from the pop-up menu that appears, choose Export Song List. A Save dialog will appear, so choose where you want to save the file on your hard disk, then click Save. iTunes exports your playlist as a tab-delimited text file, which you can open with a spreadsheet or database program like Microsoft Excel, FileMaker Pro, etc., and then print out the file.

Combining Two Playlists into One

If you realize that you have two similar playlists (like one called Big-Hair Rock and '80s Monster Rock), you can combine them into one playlist (which you could name Big-Hair '80s Monster Rock) by simply clicking-and-dragging one playlist onto another playlist, right within the Source list. Now, it's important to note that dragging the Big-Hair Rock playlist into the '80s Monster Rock playlist creates a combined playlist (copying one playlist into another, which by the way will cause any duplicate songs that were in both lists to appear twice, so you may want to delete the duplicates). Luckily, iTunes doesn't erase the Big-Hair Rock playlist. It's still there—with all its Night Ranger rockness.

Finding the Length of Your Playlist

Want to know how long (in days, hours, minutes, etc.) one of your playlists is (or for that matter, how long it would take to play your entire music Library)? Click on any playlist (or your Library), and then look at the bottom center of your iTunes window. You'll see how many songs are in your selected playlist, and how long it would take to play them all. If you actually click on the time, you can toggle between a generic hour timeframe or see it spelled out for you in hours, minutes, and seconds.

---

iTip

Be sure to make note of the playlist's total size. This really comes in handy when burning playlists to CDs, because this little nugget of info will save you a ton of frustration by allowing you to estimate the total size of your files before you even begin the burning process. (Note: Keep in mind that the total size listed is for your compressed files, not the uncompressed AIF files that'll automatically be burned onto the audio CD; hence the word estimate.)

Putting Your Songs in Your Order

There are a number of different ways to have iTunes automatically sort the songs in one of your playlists (e.g., alphabetically by Song Name or Artist, by Genre, Rating, etc.), but what if you want to arrange the songs manually so they're in *your* order? You can do it by simply dragging the songs into the order you want, but this "drag-and-drop" arranging can only be done within playlists, not in your main Library. Also, to sort the songs manually like this, you have to click in the very first column header from the left to make it the active column (it's called the Track Number column, but its name doesn't appear); otherwise, if one of the other columns (like Artist) is highlighted, the songs will already be auto-sorted by artist, right? Right! So click in the far-left column, and then you can begin sorting. Oh yeah, one last thing—if you have the Shuffle option turned on (the second button from the left at the bottom-left corner of the iTunes window), it won't let you manually sort. So if you're in a playlist, and you've got the first column highlighted, and you still can't sort, it's probably because Shuffle is turned on. Turn it off by clicking on the Shuffle button, and you're in business.

Rearranging Your Column Order

If you're not happy with the default order of the columns (for example, if you'd prefer that the My Rating column was the third column right after Song Name), you can make it happen. Just click-and-hold the My Rating column's header and drag it to the left, until it appears right after the Song Name column (you'll see a "ghost" image of your column as you move it, so it's pretty simple to move it where you want it). Now that you know how it's done, you can arrange the columns in any order you want (except for the Track Number and Song Name columns—those are stuck there permanently; besides those two, though, you can arrange your columns any way you want).

Rating Your Songs (and Why You Should)

Even though you probably like all the songs you've imported into iTunes (or you wouldn't have imported them, right?), there are some songs in your Library that you like better than others. In fact, there are probably some of your all-time favorites, some you like pretty well, and some you just like okay. Well, you can—and should—give each song a rating (using a one- to five-star rating system). One reason to rate songs is that once you've given songs a high rating (four or five stars), iTunes automatically adds your top-rated songs into a default Smart Playlist named My Top Rated (depending on your version of iTunes). So anytime you want to hear just your favorite songs, there's already a playlist (that updates live) ready for you. Plus, you can sort your songs using the My Rating column (by just clicking on it), and you can create your own custom Smart Playlists based on your ratings (see next page). To rate a song, just click directly on the song, then click in the left-hand side of the My Rating column (found in the main iTunes window) and drag to the right. As you drag, stars will highlight, so click until you see the first star and drag to the right until the fifth star is "lit." To "unlight" a star, drag back to the left. You can also rate by Control-clicking (PC: Right-clicking) on a song, and then choosing your rating from the contextual menu. *Note:* If you're on a Mac, you can even rate the song that's playing from the Mac's Dock by clicking-and-holding on the iTunes Dock icon and choosing your rating from there; on a Windows PC, Right-click the iTunes icon in the Navigation Area on the Taskbar and choose My Rating.

Putting Your Ratings to Work

Now that you've rated your songs, here's how to create a Smart Playlist using those rat-ings: Since iTunes automatically creates a Smart Playlist of your top-rated songs, why not create a playlist of your 25 lowest-rated songs (just for the sheer variety of it)? To do that, choose New Smart Playlist from the iTunes File menu, and in the dialog that appears, from the first pop-up menu choose My Rating; from the second menu choose Is Less Than; and click in the third field to choose two stars, then click OK. That's it—you have a new Smart Playlist of nothing but your lowest-rated songs. Oh, ensure the Live Updating checkbox is turned on (it should be on by default), and as you rate new songs with a one- or two-star rating, they'll be added to this Smart Playlist automatically.

---

iTip

Since iTunes tracks so much information about your songs and about your song-playing habits (it knows which songs you've played the most, the rankings of those songs, etc.), iTunes can make Smart Playlists based on these stats or based on your own personal pref-erences. What's cool is that Smart Playlists feature live updating, so if you make a change (like playing a song, changing the rating of a song, or playing a song a bunch), these Smart Playlists update automatically. But the real power comes when you create your own Smart Playlists, which also can update automatically if you'd like. Once you make your own—even once—the power of Smart Playlists will become clear, my young apprentice.

Using Genres to Create a Smart Playlist

Once you've assigned custom genres to your iTunes songs, you can make some wicked Smart Playlists. For example, I wanted to create a "car mix" that would be the equivalent of a radio station that played nothing but my songs, in random order, with no commercials. But I didn't want it to include my son's songs (I let him have a playlist on my iPod), or any Christmas songs, or any songs I use in video editing, or…well, you get the idea. So I made a Smart Playlist by holding the Option key (PC: Alt key), then clicking on the Create a Playlist button in the bottom left-hand corner of the iTunes window. This brings up the Smart Playlist dialog. At the top, under Match All of the Following Conditions, I chose Genre from the first pop-up menu. From the second menu, I chose Is Not, then in the text field I entered the genre I didn't want ("Christmas Songs"). I then clicked on the Plus Sign button to the right of the field to add another condition. I chose the same pop-up menus, and in the field I entered "Jordan's Music." I did it again for "Video Background Music," "Conference Music," and "Radio Disney Mix." Then I finally ensured Live Updating was turned on, and when I clicked OK, my "Car Mix" Smart Playlist was created, without any of the songs I didn't want. Now when I add a new song (that's labeled with any other genre than the ones I blocked), it's automatically added to my Car Mix Smart Playlist.

Create a Smart Playlist of Your Least-Played Songs

If you have thousands of songs on your iPod (or even hundreds for that matter), there are probably tunes on there that you haven't listened to much. Want a great idea for a Smart Playlist? Have iTunes create one made up of songs you haven't played recently (or at all). Start by holding the Option key (PC: Alt key) and clicking on the Create a Playlist button in the bottom-left corner of the iTunes window. When the Smart Playlist dialog appears, under Match the Following Condition, from the first pop-up menu choose Play Count. From the second menu, choose Is Less Than, and then in the blank field type "3" (or however many times you'd like, but keep it a low number). Make sure Live Updating is turned on, then click OK. A new Smart Playlist will be created of your least-played songs, and as you hear these songs more than three times (or however many times you specified), they'll automatically drop off the Smart Playlist, thanks to the Live Updating option. You could also do a variation on this by choosing Last Played in the first field, choosing Is Before in the second field, then in the text field entering a date from a few months back. When you click OK, iTunes will create a Smart Playlist made up of songs you haven't heard in months.

A Smart Playlist for Short Trips

If you only live ten minutes from your job (lucky you), you probably don't want to listen to one long song all the way to work, right? So why not create a Smart Playlist of just short songs? Here's how: Option-click (PC: Alt-click) on the Create a Playlist button to create a Smart Playlist. When the dialog appears, from the first pop-up menu choose Time; from the second pop-up menu choose Is Less Than; and in the text field enter "3:00." Now, when you play this Smart Playlist on your iPod on the way to work, you'll hear around three full songs, and you'll be at least one-third of the way through the fourth.

---

iTip

Want another Smart Playlist idea? How about this one—want to hear the same songs you heard exactly one week ago? Well, when you create your Smart Playlist, in the first pop-up menu, choose Last Played; in the second menu choose Is; and in the text field enter the date exactly one week ago today. A new Smart Playlist will be created with just the songs you heard exactly seven days ago. By the way, you might as well name this Smart Playlist "Déjà Vu." Hey, it's just an idea.

Get This Party Started with Party Shuffle

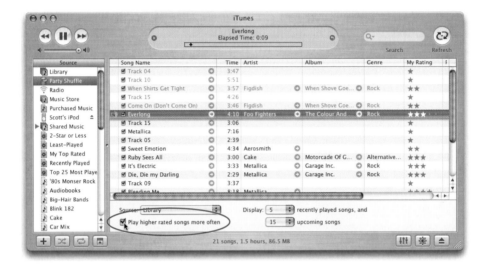

Another cool iTunes feature Apple added back in 2004 is the Party Shuffle. Rather than just choosing random songs (as the regular Shuffle command does), Party Shuffle is more likely to play songs that you've ranked highly or that you play often, so basically it plays more of your favorite songs than a standard random shuffle would. In fact, you can pretty much force Party Shuffle to favor your highly-rated songs by clicking on Party Shuffle in the Source list on the left side of the iTunes window. When the Party Shuffle options appear at the bottom of the iTunes window, choose Play Higher Rated Songs More Often. But your "party control" doesn't end there. Other differences between Party Shuffle and a regular shuffle include: You can see what's already been played; you can see what's coming up next; and you have lots of control over it. You can choose to skip a song, delete it, move it higher in the playlist, etc., using the controls at the bottom of the iTunes window. So, Party Shuffle compiles the songs into a list, but as "party DJ," you really have the final say as to what gets played and when.

Party Shuffling from a Playlist

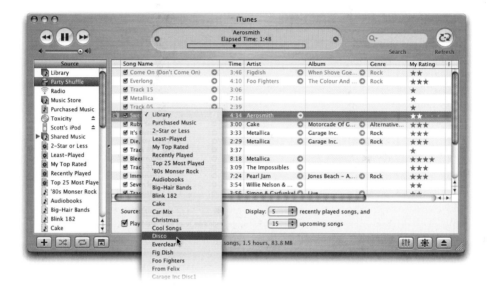

This is a great way to save time when you're making a Party Shuffle: Base the new shuffle on a preexisting playlist. For example, instead of the default of having Party Shuffle just pull random songs from your Library, have it pull from just a particular playlist. So let's say that you're having a theme party (like disco night); you can have Party Shuffle be the DJ by pulling random songs from your Disco playlist. Here's how it's done: When you click on Party Shuffle, the shuffled songs appear in the main window, but if you look at the bottom of the list (where the Party Shuffle controls now appear), you'll see a Source pop-up menu (which by default is set to Library). Choose the playlist you want to base your Party Shuffle on from this list, and you're set.

Smart Playlist Idea for DJs

Let's say you're going to be the DJ at a party next week using your iPod. Obviously, you're going to need a lot of dance songs, but you're also going to need a playlist of slow songs. Using a Smart Playlist, you can gather all the slow songs you need pretty quickly. Just go through your Library and Command-click (PC: Control-click) on every slow song you think you might want to use. Once you've gotten all the slow songs selected, press Command-I (PC: Control-I) to bring up the Multiple Song Information dialog and click on the Info tab. In the Comments field, type in the words "Slow Songs" and click OK to add that comment to each selected song. Now, go under the File menu and choose New Smart Playlist. When the Smart Playlist dialog appears, from the first pop-up menu choose Comment, in the second menu choose Is, and in the text field enter "Slow Songs." Click OK and all the slow songs will be in their own playlist. Now do the same for all your dance songs—add the comment "Dance Songs" to each one, then make a Dance Songs Smart Playlist the same way.

Smart Playlist Idea: No Explicit Lyrics

If you have a playlist that holds a lot of current music, you can almost bet that some songs are going to have explicit lyrics (Apple warns which iTunes Music Store songs have explicit lyrics by putting the word "Explicit" in red beside the song's name). For example, there are explicit lyrics on songs from the most recent albums from well-known artists like Green Day, Janet Jackson, Eminem, Nelly, and Pearl Jam, and if some of these artists are your favorites, then it's likely you've downloaded some songs with explicit lyrics. Now, although you might enjoy these lyrics (sicko), you might not want these explicit songs blaring from your car stereo when your 7-year-old is in the backseat. The solution? A Smart Playlist of your favorite songs that automatically excludes any songs with explicit lyrics. The first step is "tagging" your songs with a keyword when you download them. When you download an explicit song, immediately click on the song, press Command-I (PC: Control-I) and in the Get Info dialog, click on the Info tab. In the Comments field, type the word "Explicit," and then click OK. Now go under the File menu and choose New Smart Playlist. When the dialog appears, from the first pop-up menu choose Playlist, in the second menu choose Is, and in the third menu choose the playlist with all your favorite songs (including the ones with explicit lyrics). Then click the Plus Sign button to add another line of criteria. In the first pop-up menu choose Comments, in the second menu choose Does Not Contain, and in the text field type "Explicit." Now click OK to create a new playlist with all your favorite songs, except the ones with explicit lyrics.

Smart Playlist Idea: Good '80s Songs Instantly

Okay, you want a list of nothing but your favorite songs from the 1980s. Here's what you do: Go under the File menu and choose New Smart Playlist. When the dialog appears, in the first pop-up menu choose Year; in the second pop-up menu choose Is In The Range; and in the two fields to the right enter 1980 and 1989. Then click the Plus Sign button to add another line of criteria. From the first pop-up menu choose My Rating; in the second pop-up menu choose Is Greater Than; in the star field choose three stars; and then click OK. Now you've got a playlist of just the songs in your iTunes Library published during the '80s, but since they have a four-star or higher rating, it's just your highest-rated (favorite) songs. Not bad, eh?

---

iTip

Want to hear a playlist of just your latest music? It's Smart Playlist time—go under the File menu and choose New Smart Playlist. When the dialog appears, from the first pop-up menu choose Date Added; from the second choose Is In The Last; in the text field enter 30; choose Days in the fourth pop-up menu; and click OK. A new Smart Playlist will appear with only your newest songs. If you want to tweak it even more (so this new list is made up of only your highest-rated new songs), click the Plus Sign button to add another line of criteria, and then from the first pop-up menu choose My Rating; in the second menu choose Is Greater Than; in the star field choose four stars; and then click OK.

Smart Playlist Idea: Your Real Top 100

Here's a great way to put together a real list of your favorite songs (which may even include songs you didn't know were your real favorites). Go under the File menu and choose New Smart Playlist. When the dialog appears, from the first pop-up menu choose Play Count; from the second menu choose Is Greater Than; and in the text field enter "20." Then turn on the Limit To checkbox, enter "100," and choose Songs. Now click OK and a new Smart Playlist will appear, consisting of only your most frequently played songs—your real top 100.

Chapter Nine

Proof of Purchase

Using the iTunes Music Store

Apple changed the music industry forever when it introduced the iTunes Music Store with its "fair play" technology, which preserves the rights of the artists who make their music available for legal download. It was revolutionary, and more importantly, it worked. Now more than a million songs are available for legal download from the ITMS. I call it the ITMS because writing out "iTunes Music Store" each time I mention it gets really old really fast. Not just for me, mind you, but for you—the reader. That's why acronyms exist. People get tired of reading, writing, and even saying long names. For example, my full legal name (as it appears on my birth certificate) is Stephen Charles Oscar Theodore Thaddeus Kevin Edward Lawrence Bradley Young. After painstakingly writing it out that way for more than 26 years, I finally came up with the acronym SCOTT KELBY instead, which is much easier to write, and best of all, its meaning is pretty obvious to your average person (kind of like IBM or UPS). For the next three years, I always wrote the acronym in all caps, but once I realized that most people knew what it stood for (like ASAP or NFL), I then dropped the cap on everything but the first letter of each word, making it just Scott Kelby. Now, about the name of this chapter—it's actually a band's name, Proof of Purchase, and (as of the writing of this book) you can find two of their songs on the ITMS. I listened to the 30-second ITMS preview of their song "Fallacy," and it scared the livin' crap out of me. Don't ever listen to that preview with the lights out. It's way too Eerie, Creepy, and Scary. It's ECS.

Navigating the ITMS

When you click on the Music Store in the Source list of the iTunes window, iTunes will take you to the iTunes Music Store (ITMS for short). Luckily, the store is a lot like a website, in that there's a homepage (the main page you see when you launch the ITMS). If you search for a song or click on an album on the homepage, iTunes takes you to the page for that song and the navigation for ITMS kicks in. You can always get back to the homepage anytime by clicking on the little Home button that appears near the top-left corner of the iTunes main window. If you want to navigate back to the previous page, just press the Back button (to the left of the Home button). In fact, if you ever get lost, just look to the right of the Home button, and you'll see little tabs that show exactly how deep into the store you are. These are clickable, so if you want to jump back to one of those tabs (such as the genre), just click on it.

---

iTip

Just like a Web browser, you can return to your previous page by using keyboard short-cuts. For example, to jump back one page, press Command-[(PC: Control-[). That's the Left Bracket key—it's immediately to the right of the letter P on your keyboard. To jump forward one page, press Command-] (PC: Control-])—that's the Right Bracket key.

The Homepage Navigation Dots

On the homepage of the ITMS, there are special areas for new releases and ITMS exclusives, and although only four CD covers are visible, there are actually more, and you can scroll to see them by clicking the blue circular arrow buttons on the left and right of each area. What's cool is that Apple added a little visual navigation area so you know how deep you've dug into the list of new releases, exclusives, or pre-releases. It's those four little round buttons at the top center of each section. Not only do they show you where you are in the scrolling list, you can click on them to jump directly to a panel of CDs (so if you wanted to jump to the fourth set, you'd click on the fourth little circle and you'd jump right there). To get back to the original homepage set, click on the first circle again. See, it's the little things, isn't it?

---

iTip

Want to take a quick look at what's been added to the ITMS recently? Of course, you could scroll through the featured New Releases section or navigate using the four little dots at the top of the New Releases box. But if you use the following shortcut, you'll be able to see what's new this week, last week, the week before that, and the week before that. That's right, instead of clicking on the left or right blue arrow just click right on the words "See All" in the upper right–hand corner of the New Releases box. A page will appear that lists everything that's been new for the last four weeks. Nice.

You Can Browse in the ITMS Too!

Genre browsing really works well in the ITMS because everything has a genre attached to it. So, if you want to browse through all the Comedy tracks, just click on the Browse button in the top-right corner, then in the Genre list on the left, click on Comedy. All the comedians that have downloadable tracks will then appear in the Artist list (in the top center), and if you click on an artist, all of his or her albums appear along the top-right side. Click on an album, and those tracks will appear in the main window. *Warning:* If you try this a few times in the ITMS, you'll most likely love it, and then you'll start using genre browsing in your own Library, even though you thought you didn't like browsing. Hey, I'm just sayin'.

---

iTip

There's more to the ITMS than meets the eye, because almost everything you see is a clickable link. So if you do a search and some album covers appear at the top of the window, try moving your cursor over the text beside an album—like over the artist's name. It'll highlight with a link that'll take you not just to the album, but to all that artist's work. By the way, you can even click on the Explicit warning text, and you'll get a detailed description of just what "explicit" means. Just in case you were wondering, it means "really naughty stuff."

Making Your Searches Make Sense

When you get the results of a search, they are listed in order of their relevance to the song name (or artist, etc.) you entered. However, that doesn't mean the song you want is on top—quite the contrary—so I usually wind up re-sorting these results by something else to help me find the song I'm looking for. Here's an example: I'm searching for the song "Mexico" (the Jimmy Buffett version), but when I type "Mexico" in the Search field, there are 250 results, and the one iTunes chose as the most relevant (sorted by Song Name) was "57 Miles from Mexico" by Steve White. So what's the quickest way for me to find the Buffett version? Click on the Artist column, which re-sorts these results alphabetically by artist, sending Steve White to the bottom of the list, and Jimmy Buffett closer to the top (since it sorts by the first name, I have to scroll down to the J's, but it'll still be faster and easier to find him).

---

iTip

Since there are more than one million songs on the ITMS, you can bet there are multiple versions of certain songs (even multiple versions by the same artist—the live version, the unplugged version, etc.), and finding the right version of your song may take listening to a lot of 30-second previews. However, you can speed things up by using this trick: Once the list of matching songs appears, double-click the first song in the list, and the moment you realize that it's not the version you want, just hit the Right Arrow key on your keyboard and the next version's preview will play. Keep hittin' that Right Arrow until you find the right version. This is one huge timesaving shortcut!

Can't Find It? Try a Power Search!

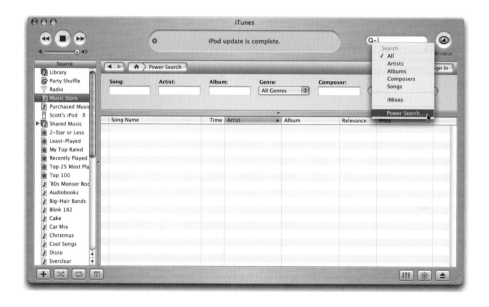

If the regular ITMS Search feature doesn't do the trick for you (maybe you're looking for some really obscure song and just aren't finding it, but you figure it's probably there somewhere—maybe you don't have the correct spelling of the artist's name, or something like that), you can try a Power Search, which lets you really refine your criteria. To do a Power Search, click-and-hold the Magnifying Glass icon that appears on the left side of the regular Search field and choose Power Search from the pop-up menu that appears. A more detailed search area will appear across the top of your main window. Now you can search in multiple areas (like Song, Artist, Album, Genre, and/or Composer) all at once. Hey, it's worth a try.

---

iTip

If you've searched the ITMS and the song you want just isn't available yet, what can you do? Tell Apple. That's right, Apple has a music request form so you can tell them which songs you'd like to see added to the iTunes Music Store. To find this online form, visit www.apple.com/feedback/itunes.html and when you get there, from the Feedback Type pop-up menu choose Music Requests, then in the Comments field tell them the name of the song(s) and the artist(s) you'd like to see added. It's no guarantee, but if you want it badly enough to let Apple know, you're probably not alone, and the more times they hear it, the better chance you'll soon find it on the ITMS. Give it a shot.

Finding Songs from When You Graduated

Remember all those great songs from the year you graduated high school? Neither do I. Well, I remember them if I hear them or see their names, but off the top of my head, I can only name a handful. That's why it's so cool that the ITMS has *Billboard* magazine's Hot 100 charts dating back to 1946, so all you have to do is find the one for the year you graduated from school, and 100 songs that sound really bad today will be listed (hey, don't laugh, when I graduated, the No. 1 song was "Shadow Dancing" by Andy Gibb). You can view *Billboard's* Hot 100 charts (and buy the songs listed on them) by starting at the ITMS homepage and clicking on Billboard Charts in the list of categories on the left of the window. This brings up a Charts browser. In the Genre section click on Charts; in the Charts section click on *Billboard* Hot 100; and then in the Years section click on the year you graduated. (I'm not telling you what year I graduated, but it could've been 1994. Hey, it could've been—if I had been a really, really, really bad student.) *Warning:* When you click on your year, you'll see a list of songs that will immediately elicit the following exclamation: "Oh no way that song was No. 1."

Quickly Finding All of an Artist's Songs

If you see an artist you'd like to see more of (let's say you're searching for songs, and you happen to see a Willie Nelson song in the results—hey, Willie rocks), just click on the little gray circle with an arrow inside it right after the artist's name. Clicking on this takes you directly to a page where you'll find all of the artist's songs available on the ITMS. Some artists even have a "feature page" that will appear when you click on the little arrow; then you not only get the big fancy photo of the artist(s), but if you look around on this page you're also likely to find a Biography link. Click on it and get some background info on the artist, a complete discography, etc. Hey, it saves you a trip to the artist's website. Try this once, and you'll use it again and again.

Emailing Your Uncovered Treasures

If you've just uncovered the coolest song on the ITMS, you can send a friend directly to that song. Just open your email program (while you still have the ITMS visible), and click-and-drag the song's album cover (or the song title, either will work) over into your opened email message. The song's ITMS URL will be pasted into your email, just like a regular Web link. All your friend has to do is click on that link, and she'll be taken right there. This is a great feature to use when your girlfriend/boyfriend breaks up with you. You can send her links to a bunch of "broken-hearted" breakup songs, like "Here With You" by 3 Doors Down or "What Happened To Us?" by Hoobastank or the most obvious "The Breakup Song" by Greg Kihn—but I'm not sure that song will have the desired effect (the song name is good, but the message is weak if you're trying to get some broken-hearted sympathy).

Finding Out if You Already Have a Song

Okay, you're checking out some music on the iTunes Music Store and you come across a song you really like (let's say it's "Vertigo" by U2), and you say to yourself, "Ya know, I really like that song. I wonder—do I already have it?" Well, wonder no more, because here's a very slick and very fast way to find out—hold the Option key (PC: Alt key) and click on the little gray arrow to the right of the artist's name in the ITMS. This jumps you out of the ITMS and directly to a list of the U2 songs in *your* Library, so you can see if you've got it. Seriously, how cool is that? It leaves the Music Store and shows you which U2 songs you've already got in *your* Library. I just think that's so cool (try it once and you'll see what I mean).

Seeing The Big Cover!

If you buy songs from the iTunes Music Store, there's a little bonus: Not only does it download the album art (so you can see it in the left-hand corner of the iTunes interface when you click the Song Artwork button—it's the fourth button from the left), but if you click directly on the album art, a separate floating window will appear with a huge version of the cover. Well, technically you could get either a huge or a medium version, depending on how long it's been since you downloaded the song from the ITMS, because the super-huge, almost-full-screen covers are a new feature. Either way, it's fairly cool to see the covers at a much larger size.

---

iTip

You can actually have more than one album cover per song (meaning there's an import cover, or an extended mix cover, or single cover, etc.). Just drag the cover you want from your Web browser (that means you found the album cover on the band's website) and drop it right over the cover that's there now. You'll notice little arrows will appear above your album art, so you can cycle over to see the different covers.

Why You Need to Back Up Your Purchased Songs

In the back of your mind you're probably thinking, "Hey, if my hard drive ever totally dies, I'm covered, because Apple keeps a history of all my iTunes purchases, and if that mega-crash day ever comes, I'll just drop Apple an email and they'll let me download all the purchased songs again, right?" Nope. If your hard drive dies, all of your purchased songs go right to the grave with it. Apple will *not* let you download them again without paying for them. That's why it's SO important to back up your purchased music. To do this, first click on Purchased Music in the Source list (on the left side of the iTunes window) to select it. Then click on the Burn Disc button in the top right-hand corner of the iTunes window. Insert a blank disc (when iTunes tells you to), then start-a-burnin'. Keep poppin' in new discs until all those songs are backed up to CD. Now, will Apple ever change its mind about this, since serious hard disk crashes are nearly an inevitability? Probably one day, but it hasn't happened yet, and until it does, you're not "covered." If you don't back up, one day you're almost certain to lose your entire ITMS investment. So…back it up now (step away from the book and start backing up).

A Source for Musical Inspiration

If you can't think of any songs to buy and you need a little inspiration, go to the ITMS homepage, and on the left side of the main window, scroll down and click on Celebrity Playlists. Apple has asked a number of well-known celebrities (mostly musicians) to create and publish their own playlists, and often their suggestions for songs are very good. You can sort the listing by date added (to get the most recent celebrity play-lists) or alphabetically by name using the pop-up menu in the top-right corner of the ITMS window. Once you find a musician or celebrity that interests you, just click on that person's photo to see his picks and, most importantly, a note on why he picked 'em. Best of all, because his picks are sold on the ITMS, you can hear a 30-second preview of each suggestion. This may sound a little corny, but if you give it a try, I think you'll be quite surprised at some of the cool music your favorite celebrities and bands are listening to.

---

iTip

Since Apple introduced iMix (which basically makes you the celebrity), you can publish your own playlists on the iTunes Music Store and share them with the world (so other people can buy your favorite songs). To create and publish your own iMix, just put together a playlist of your favorite songs within iTunes, then go under the File menu and choose Create an iMix. iTunes will connect to the Music Store and your iMix will be live. To see other people's iMixes (and rate them), go to the ITMS homepage and click on iMix on the left side of the window.

Controlling Your Spending

With songs being only 99¢, they just seem so cheap that it's easy to buy songs—until the VISA bill comes and you're shocked at how many 99¢ charges there are. Rather than just blindly buying songs one at a time, turn on the ITMS's Shopping Cart feature. Go to the iTunes Preferences (under the iTunes menu on the Mac; under the Edit menu on a Windows PC). Just click on the Store tab in the dialog, and then choose Buy Using a Shopping Cart. This changes the Buy Song button to Add Song. Now when you click the Add Song button, songs will wind up listed on your Shopping Cart page at check-out time. None of these songs is downloaded or charged to your account until you actually press the Buy Now button at the bottom of your Shopping Cart page. To go back to your freewheeling, spend-like-a-drunken-sailor ways, return to the Store Preferences and check Buy and Download Using 1-Click.

---

iTip

Let's say you found some songs on the iTunes Music Store that you want to buy, but you just don't have money right now. Well, although the iTunes Music Store doesn't have a "Wish List" feature, try this: Create a folder on your desktop named "ITMS Wish List." Then, when you find a song (or a whole album) that you want to add to your Wish List, just click-and-drag the song or album cover into that folder on your desktop. The location of that song or album on the ITMS is embedded into a document, so just double-click on that document and the ITMS will launch and take you to that song or album.

Keeping a Tab on Your Spending

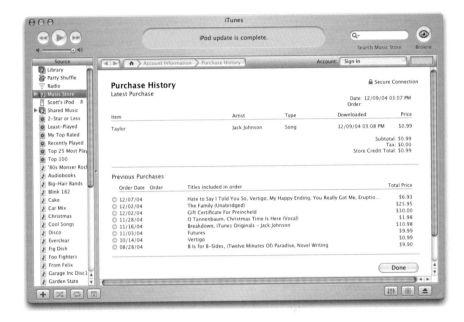

Although Apple knows exactly how much money you've been spending recently at the ITMS, you might want to know yourself (so you can prepare items that will need to be pawned). To find out how much you've spent, just click on the Account button (the one that shows your email address) in the upper right-hand corner of the ITMS. Even if you're already logged in, it'll ask you for your password again (just as a precaution). Once you enter your password, click on the View Account button to bring up your Account Info page. There you'll find a button called Purchase History. Click it and get ready to freak out as all the purchases, and their costs, are listed one after another. When you've wiped away your tears, press the Done button, because "you're done."

---

iTip

If you're using the ITMS at work, and you duck out for lunch, someone else might want to duck into your office, buy a few songs on your dime, download them to his iPod, and then head back to his cubicle before you return. You won't know what happened until your VISA bill arrives. So, when you know you're stepping away for a few minutes, click on the Account button (the one that shows your email) at the top right of the ITMS window and choose Sign Out from the dialog that appears. That way, no one can come in and abuse your account while you're out. When you come back, just log back in and continue downloading more songs on company time.

Setting Up an iTunes Allowance

Want a high-tech way to spoil your kids? How about giving them an ITMS download allowance? It's scarily convenient, because once you choose how much they get each month, it's all automated from there: The ITMS credits their account each month and charges your credit card—it's downright eerie. Now, although I'm poking some fun at it here, when you think about it, this is much safer than giving them your (or their own) credit card, because *you* determine exactly how much they can spend. Here's how to set your kids up: From the ITMS homepage, in the list of links on the left side, click on Allowance. This brings up the Allowance setup page, where you can give your child an allowance of up to $200 a month. (By the way, if you choose $200, your next call should be to a therapist.) Once you've entered your information, click Continue. When you sign in to your account, Apple will deliver the "good news" to your children. How personal and folksy.

---

iTip

Another of my favorite iTunes Music Store features is the ability to email or mail a friend a gift certificate for buying songs there. Just go to the iTunes Music Store, sign in, and click on Gift Certificates. Then you'll have your choice of buying gift certificates or (if you're lucky) redeeming one. If you're redeeming one, the ITMS will give you credits in the amount of the gift certificate, and your running balance will appear in the right-hand corner of the ITMS window. By the way, you can buy certificates in person at the Apple Store in the mall, too.

Stop Unauthorized People from Buying Music

The songs you download from the iTunes Music Store can be copied to just five computers (thanks to a built-in digital rights protection scheme called "Fair Play"), so theoretically, you could buy a song on your desktop machine, then authorize your laptop as your second machine, and then authorize your computer at work as your third, and you'd still have two computers left to authorize (plus you can copy songs to as many of your iPods as you'd like—fair enough). You can also buy more songs from these five machines and charge them to your account. But that also means if you sell your computer or give it to someone else (maybe someone else within your company will wind up using your old machine), you definitely want to "deauthorize" it, or they may be able to buy songs too—and charge them to you. To deauthorize your computer, go under the Advanced menu in iTunes and choose Deauthorize Computer. When the dialog appears, click OK and the computer you're currently using will be deactivated. *Note:* Just erasing and reformatting a hard drive will not deauthorize a computer—you have to deauthorize it manually as shown here.

Sharing ITMS Music

If you're on a network (at work, at home, at school, etc.), you can share your playlists with other people on the network. That's right; they can play the songs in your playlists from right within their copy of iTunes. The only downside is that they won't get to hear songs you bought from the iTunes Music Store—when those purchased songs appear in a playlist, iTunes skips over them automatically (to, once again, protect the copyrights of the music you bought). If you want someone on your network to be able to hear your ITMS music, you'll have to "authorize" his computer. Just go to his computer, log in with your ITMS user name (email address) and password, then go under the Advanced menu and choose Authorize Computer. (*Note:* This computer then becomes one of the five that you're allowed to authorize under your ITMS account.)

Speeding Up Sharing and Previews

If you're on a local network, chances are you've got a direct and pretty speedy connection to that network. If that's the case, you can speed things up even more by tweaking an iTunes preference that will accelerate the loading of both the ITMS previews and the shared playlists across your network. What you're doing is just shrinking the iTunes Streaming Buffer Size, meaning it buffers a smaller amount of info before it begins playing, so you see previews faster and hear shared songs faster. If that all sounds confusing, it should. So, does it really matter what kind of magic goes into making iTunes run faster? No? Then great, do this: Go to iTunes Preferences (found under the iTunes menu on a Mac; the Edit menu on a Windows PC), then click on the Advanced tab. From the pop-up menu for Streaming Buffer Size, choose Small, and now things will move faster. See, that was fairly painless, eh, Bunky?

Got a Slow Connection? Get Better Previews

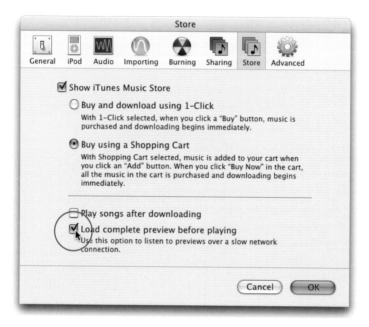

If you have a slow-speed (dial-up) connection to the Internet, you're probably suffering a frustrating version of one of the coolest ITMS features—the ability to hear a 30-second preview of any song. The problem is that these previews stream, and because of the slow speed of your dial-up connection, those audio streams often skip, are choppy, and sometimes are out-and-out painful to listen to. But it doesn't have to be that way. Just buy a high-speed connection! (Kidding.) Actually, there's something you can do—stop the streaming. That's right, there's a preference that stops the streaming audio and instead loads the entire music preview before it plays. That way, there's no chopping and no skipping—just clean, pure previews, baby! Here's how to turn it on: Go to the iTunes Preferences (on a Mac, it's under the iTunes menu; on a Windows PC, it's under the Edit menu) and when the dialog appears, click on the Store tab. Then turn on the checkbox labeled Load Complete Preview Before Playing. That's it—it'll take a little extra time while the preview is downloading, but once it does, it'll sound perfect. *Note:* Turn on this option only if you're using a telephone line dial-up connection. If you have a cable modem, T1, or DSL connection, you should leave this turned off.

Putting ITMS Links on Your Website

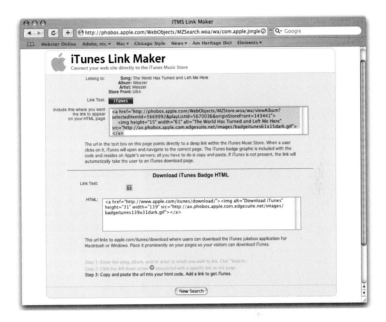

If you've got a blogging website (or any personal website for that matter) and you want to lead other people to a song on the ITMS, Apple is delighted to let you do just that! So delighted, in fact, that Apple will even create the HTML code you need so you can paste it right into your HTML page, using Apple's iTunes Link Maker. You start by going to www.apple.com/itunes/linkmaker and from there you can enter the song name, album name, or artist name, then click on the Search button. If you see your song in the search results, just click on the gray circular arrow beside it and you'll be taken to a page with the HTML code in place, ready for you to copy and paste into the HTML coding on your site.

---

iTip

Want to take a peek at what the iTunes Music Store for Germany is like? Easy enough—just start at the ITMS homepage, and on the left side of the main window, right near the top, click on the link for Choose Store and a page will appear with gel-looking buttons representing each of the iTunes Music Stores in the world. To see what another country's store is like (and to see its top songs), just click on one of the buttons.

Chapter Ten
Tip Drill
Cool iTunes Tips

You'd think "Tip Drill" for a chapter about iTunes tips is just about as perfect a name as you can come up with. It totally makes sense, plus it's the name of a song from Nelly, and it's the name of a DVD documentary (which features—and was inspired by—the Nelly song of the same name). Now, being the NFL football fan that I am (Go Bucs!), when I hear "tip drill," I think of a practice drill in which a passed ball gets "tipped" by a member of the defense, making that ball much easier to intercept. NFL teams practice these tip drills all the time, and that's why in a real game, when a pass gets tipped, everybody holds their breath, because it's probably going to be intercepted. So, when I came across a song named "Tip Drill," I was drawn to it. Now, at this point it's not available from the iTunes Music Store, and that's probably a good thing because when I searched on the Web for the lyrics, I learned that "Tip Drill" is a very naughty song. In fact, it's mega-naughty. If my 8-year-old ever heard this song, there wouldn't be enough soap in the world to clear out the naughty passing through his ears. If it were available from the iTunes Music Store, I'm not sure the Explicit warning would be strong enough. It might just have to say "Yikes!" Or "Whoa, Nelly!" (Sorry, that was lame.) So, I searched for the DVD, which (not surprisingly) is about somewhat naughty things. So, to ensure that this chapter doesn't get an NC-17 rating, let's bend our song-or-movie-title-chapter-name rule and use the NFL's definition of "tip drill" instead. Thanks for understanding.

Adding Smooth Transitions Between Songs

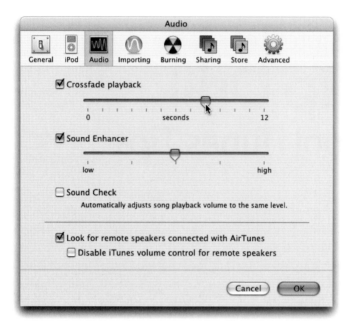

Rather than a blank gap after each song, how would you like it if when the song got near the end, it instead started fading out and the next song started fading in, just like they often do on the radio? iTunes can do this automatically—it's called "crossfading." You can add crossfading by going to the iTunes Preferences (under the iTunes menu on the Mac; under the Edit menu on a Windows PC) and clicking on the Audio icon. Next, turn on the checkbox for Crossfade Playback, and you're set. If you want a faster (or slower) crossfade between songs, you can adjust that using the Crossfade slider. The crossfades are measured in seconds, so for longer crossfades, drag the slider to the right. For shorter ones, drag to the left.

---

iTip

When you're looking for songs in your iTunes Library, you'll see lots of little gray arrows. These are actually shortcuts that lead you to more music from the same artist. Click on an arrow, and the ITMS will launch. These arrows can be very handy or very annoying, depending on your personal tolerance for little gray circles. If they're getting on your nerves, turn them off by going to iTunes' Preferences (under the iTunes menu on the Mac; under the Edit menu on a Windows PC), click on the General tab, and then turn off Show Links to Music Store. That's it—the little gray circles disappear.

Finding Your Original Songs
(for Easy Backup)

Backing up your songs is important just in case anything ever happens to your hard disk, but if you haven't consolidated all your songs into the iTunes folder (as shown in Chapter 7), finding all your original songs to back up might be quite a chore. Well, here's something that can make your life a little easier. To find the original song's location on your hard disk, just Control-click (PC: Right-click) on the song in your playlist or Library, then from the pop-up menu that appears, choose Show Song File. The folder where the song is located will appear in the foreground, making it easy to copy to a backup disk.

---

iTip

The default size for type in iTunes is fairly small, and that's cool if you're 15, but if you're older (like 18 or 19), you might want the font size a bit bigger. You can do that by going to iTunes Preferences (on the Mac, it's under the iTunes menu; on a Windows PC, it's under the Edit menu) and clicking on the General tab. You'll see pop-up menus at the top of the dialog for Source Text (the menus and such) and Song Text (the text you see in your playlists and Library). Choose Large from the pop-up menu to make the font size larger.

Editing a Song's Start/End Points

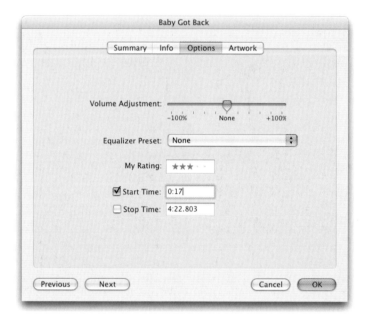

Being able to choose when a song starts (or ends) is more important than you might think. For example, the song "Baby Got Back" by Sir Mix-A-Lot starts with two Valley girls dissing some other girl's butt. It's kind of funny the first time you hear it, but by the 10th or 11th time, it really gets old. Luckily, iTunes lets you skip this part entirely by setting the Start Time for the song. Here's how: First, you need to find out exactly where in the song the "good part" starts, so play the song from the beginning and note the elapsed time when the music actually starts (in "Baby Got Back" the actual music starts 17 seconds in—the girls keep talking for a few seconds, but at least the music is playing). Now, in your Library (or playlist), Control-click (PC: Right-click) on the song you want to edit and choose Get Info from the contextual menu that appears. Click on the Options tab and you'll see checkboxes for Start Time and Stop Time. Click the Start Time checkbox, and then enter "0:17." That's it. Now when this song plays, it will skip over the Valley girls and get right to the music.

---

iTip

Here's a little button that a lot of people miss in the Get Info dialog—the Next and Previous buttons. What they do is to let you, without closing this dialog, edit the next (or previous) song in the current playlist or Library. Just click on the Next button, and the next song's info appears in this dialog, ready to edit. I know, this may not seem like the biggest deal right now, but try it a few times and you'll be surprised at how much time you'll save.

Using Album Art to Help You Navigate

By now you've noticed that when you click on a song in iTunes, that song's album art shows in the lower left-hand corner of the iTunes window (well, at least it does if you have clicked on the Show Song Artwork button in the left corner of the window—it's the fourth button in the group of four). In fact, if you look directly above the album art, you'll see the word "Selected," which means you're seeing the art for the currently selected song. But do you know that you can change the feature so that, instead of the album showing each time you click on a song, iTunes will show the cover for the song that's now playing? That's right—just click right above the album art, directly on the words "Selected Song" and it changes to "Now Playing." So, as you click on other songs, iTunes will always show you the cover for the song that's playing right now. Slick.

---

iTip

If you have an album cover that you want to apply to several songs from the same album (or a whole CD worth of songs), just Command-click (PC: Control-click) on all the songs you want to apply the album art to, then Control-click (PC: Right-click) on any song and from the contextual menu that appears, choose Get Info. Now, drag-and-drop some album art into the Artwork box, and that art will be applied to all your selected songs.

Deleting Album Art

If you have album art along with one of your songs, and you decide you want to delete that art, Control-click (PC: Right-click) on the song, and from the contextual menu that appears choose Get Info. When the dialog appears, click on the Artwork tab at the top, then click on your artwork in the preview window and the Delete button below it will activate. Click that, and it's gone! If you want to delete album art from more than one song at a time, then just Command-click (PC: Control-click) on all the songs you want to edit, press Command-I (PC: Control-I) to bring up the Multiple Song Information dialog, and click on the Artwork checkbox. The album art from all the selected songs will be deleted.

Printing Your Own CD Jewel Case Inserts

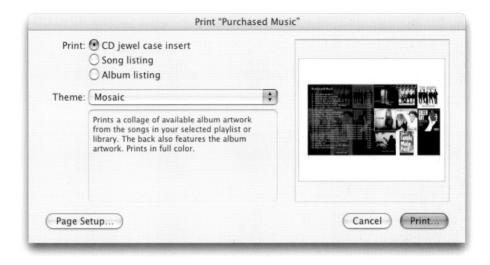

If you've burned one of your playlists to CD, you can also have iTunes print out a CD jewel case insert for you, making it easy to keep track of what's on each CD you've burned. Start by choosing which playlist you just burned to CD by clicking on it in the Source list on the left side of the iTunes dialog. Then go under File menu and choose Print. When the Print dialog appears, click on Print: CD Jewel Case Insert (if it's not already selected). iTunes will automatically compile a list of the songs in that playlist, along with their running times, and you even have a pop-up menu in which you can choose from a selection of professional-looking "themes" for your insert, including ones that include either multiple or single album covers (you'll see a preview of each right from within the Print dialog). Once you choose your theme, just click the Print button, choose your paper size or printer in the resulting dialog, and wait for your way-cool jewel case insert to spit out of the printer.

Printing Song and Album Listings

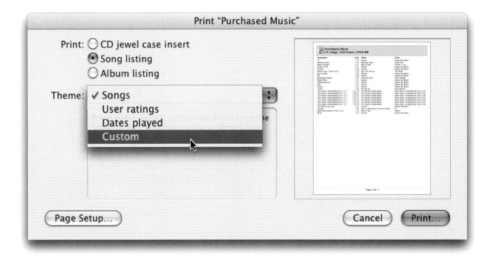

Besides printing CD jewel case inserts, iTunes also enables you to print complete lists of songs, albums, or your entire iTunes music Library (these are great to have on hand in case your computer is ever lost, stolen, or just dies a horrible grisly death). Besides just printing simple lists, you also have control over how much information is displayed on these lists. For simple playlists, you can decide if you want title, artist, album name, running time, etc., or you can ask for a layout that includes your personal ratings. You can have the list include the last date played, how many times you've played each song, or you can get a complete printout of the iTunes window view—it's all up to you (you just make your choice from the Theme pop-up menu that appears when you choose Print from the File menu, and then click on the Song Listing button). If you want a printout of all your albums, click on the Album Listing button instead, and you'll get both the album cover (if your songs have one) and a listing of which songs from that album appear in your playlist.

The Ultimate Space Saver

Mini Player on a Mac

Mini Player on a Windows PC

Once you start listening to a playlist in iTunes, there's no need to see all the tracks, the other playlists you're not playing, your Library, and basically all that other "space-stealing" stuff. To have the ultimate space-saving version of iTunes (called the iTunes Mini Player), just click once on the green Plus Sign button in the upper-left corner of the iTunes window (on a Mac), which shrinks iTunes into the Mini Player. If you're on a Windows PC, choose Switch to Mini Player from the Advanced menu (or press Control-M) to get to the Mini Player. Best of all, you still have access to the most important controls—Play, Review, Fast Forward, Volume, and Eject. To return to full size, just click the green button again (for the Mac) or click on the Maximize/Restore button (for Windows).

---

iTip

If you're using the iTunes Mini Player, it's so small that you can have it always appear in front of your other open applications (so your controls are always right there where you need them, in case the boss walks in). Just go to iTunes Preferences (under the iTunes menu on the Mac; under the Edit menu on a Windows PC), then click on the Advanced tab. When the preferences appear, turn on the checkbox for Keep Mini Player on Top of All Other Windows, and then click OK. Now, you can control iTunes without leaving your open applications.

Converting Your Songs

Here's a little-known tip for converting your imported songs to WAV format (so they can play on virtually any CD player). You start by going to iTunes Preferences (on the Mac, under the iTunes menu; on a Windows PC, under the Edit menu) and clicking on the Importing icon. Then, from the Import Using pop-up menu, choose WAV Encoder. Next, go to your playlist (or Library), hold the Command key (PC: Control key) and click on the songs you want to convert to WAV. Once they're all selected, just Control-click (PC: Right-click) on any of the selected songs and from the contextual menu that appears, choose Convert Selection to WAV. The converted versions of your songs will appear directly below each original MP3 version in your Library. By the way, if you want to save these WAV files to a different folder on your hard disk, just press-and-hold the Option key (on a Windows PC, press-and-hold the Shift key) before you choose Convert Selection to WAV from the contextual menu. This doesn't work on songs that are in the protected AAC format (like songs from the ITMS).

---

iTip

Did you know that you can set iTunes to shuffle albums randomly? So iTunes will shuffle just the albums themselves—NOT the songs on the albums. If you want to turn this feature on, just go to iTunes Preferences (under the iTunes menu on the Mac; under the Edit menu on a Windows PC) and click on the Advanced tab. Then, under Shuffle By choose Album instead of Song, and then click OK.

Moving Playlists between Computers

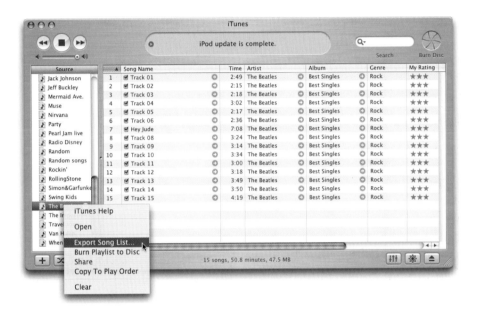

If you have more than one computer (let's say you have a desktop machine and a laptop), you probably want access to your iTunes playlists on both machines, right? Well, you could set up a wireless network, blah, blah, blah, or you could simply export your playlist from your desktop machine, and then import that playlist in iTunes on your laptop. Here's how: Just Control-click (PC: Right-click) on the playlist you want to export, then choose Export Song List from the contextual menu that appears. Now, transfer that playlist to your other computer (put it on a USB drive, burn it to CD, email it to yourself, whatever), then go under the iTunes File menu and choose Import. Locate that exported playlist file and click OK—that playlist is now in your laptop's iTunes. Ahhh, but there's a catch (you knew it couldn't be that easy, right?). What you've imported is a "list" of songs—not the songs themselves. If the songs don't already appear in the iTunes Library on the other computer, you many need to transfer the actual MP3 and AAC song files (again, you can burn them to CD or use your iPod as a hard drive [see Chapter 4 on how to do that]). Once the songs are copied onto your laptop (and placed in your iTunes Music folder), you can then use your imported playlist to hear those songs.

Sharing Your Music over a Network

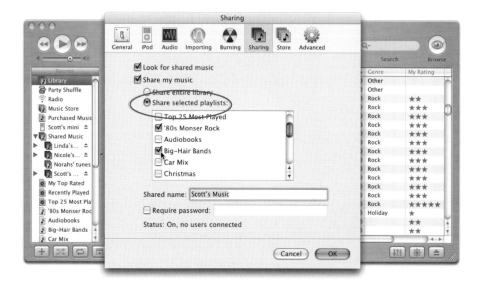

If you're connected to a network (at home, at the office, at school, etc.), you can let other people on the network listen to any (or all) of your iTunes playlists. That's right, you can reveal your own highly refined musical taste by letting other people spend some time in "your world." Best of all, setting it up takes about five seconds. First go to the iTunes Preferences (under the iTunes menu on the Mac; under the Edit menu on a Windows PC) and click on the Sharing tab. Then turn on the checkbox for Share My Music. That's it. By default, iTunes wants you to share all your music, but if you'd prefer not to share all of your playlists, then click on the Share Selected Playlists button, then from the scrolling list choose which playlists you want to be shared—just click in the empty box to put a checkmark by the ones you want to share. Click OK and you're sharing. Now, when other people on each network launch iTunes, they'll see a new listing in their Source list called "Shared Music," and under that link will be a list of people (yourself included) who are making their playlists available. They can click on your playlist, see your songs, and decide which ones they want to listen to, just as if the songs were on their own drive (but don't worry—they can't copy your songs to either their hard disk or iPod—they're just for listening only while you're sharing). (*Note:* To see their shared music, click on the Look for Shared Music checkbox in the dialog.) When you log off the network, your playlists go with you. By the way, if you only want certain people (cool people, no doubt) to be able to hear your shared lists, click the Require Password checkbox and enter a password. Then only the people you tell the password to will be allowed into your special world. What a great opportunity for you to be elitist.

iTunes Radio Is on the Air!

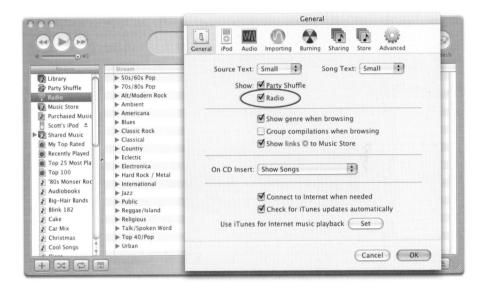

Throughout this book we've been pretty much treating iTunes as a way to organize and play your imported CDs and downloaded songs; but if you've got an Internet connection, there's another side to iTunes that they don't talk about at parties, and that's iTunes Radio. Well, it's not exactly FM radio, but instead it's a list of hundreds of streaming Internet radio stations, covering 20 different genres, broadcasting every-thing from reggae to talk shows, from metal to classical (and everything in between). The reason many people don't know about this cool hidden feature is that it's likely hidden from view in the Source list. To see the current list of stations, go to iTunes Preferences (on the Mac, it's under the iTunes menu; on a Windows PC, it's under the Edit menu) and click on the General tab. Then, under the Show category (near the top of the dialog), turn on the checkbox for Radio. Now a Radio link will appear in your Source list. Click on it to see the list of radio genres. To see the stations currently broad-casting for a particular genre, double-click the genre's name. To listen to a station, just double-click the station's name in the list.

Making Playlists of Your Favorite Stations

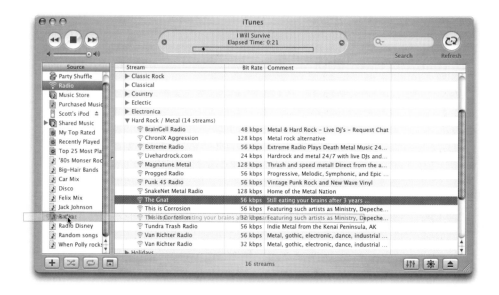

In your local FM market, there are a limited number of stations, and out of those there are probably only six or seven that you listen to often (and are programmed into the presets on your car stereo), but with iTunes streaming Internet radio, there are hundreds of stations. Even though there are hundreds, you'll still wind up picking out your favorites; it's just that you might have 28 favorites instead of only six or seven. Luckily, keeping track of your favorites is pretty easy—just put them into a playlist as if they were songs. Start by clicking the Create a Playlist button in the bottom-left corner of the iTunes window, name your playlist "Radio," then click on the Radio link in the Source list. Find the stations you like, and drag-and-drop them right onto your Radio playlist. Now the next time you want to hear them, just click on the playlist, then double-click on your favorite station to start the streaming.

---

iTip

Similar to satellite radio, many of these streaming Internet radio stations also broadcast the name and artist for the songs they play. To see the name and artist for the current song, look up in the iTunes status display. By the way, since you can log in to a station at any point in the song, the elapsed time you see displayed in the iTunes status display isn't the elapsed time for the song; it's a running count of how long you've been listening to that particular station, which could help you determine if you need to seek psychological help for a streaming-radio addiction problem.

It's Time to Get Visual

If you ever wanted a glimpse of what your parents' lives were like back when they were in their 20s, just press Command-T (PC: Control-T), which turns on iTunes' visual effects (called the Visualizer). (You can also just press the "freaky" middle button in the bottom right-hand corner of the iTunes window.) So why did Apple include these "way out" (a '60s term) visuals in iTunes? So your parents could relate to them and feel good about buying you a computer and an iPod (hey, it's possible). Anyway, the images created by the Visualizer are actually pretty cool because they react to the music you're playing in iTunes, and just watching them gives you the munchies (did I say that out loud?). *Warning:* Whatever you do, don't buy the single "Are You Experienced?" by Jimi Hendrix (from the ITMS) and have it playing while running the Visualizer as your parents are walking by your screen. They'll totally freak (and may quit their jobs).

---

iTip

Normally, the Visualizer "does its thing" by taking over your iTunes window, but we need to experience the entire trip in its full-screen splendor. So start the Visualizer (see above), press Command-F (PC: Control-F), and then sit back and stare directly into the screen. Enter into a hypnotic trance, then you can call in sick for work: "Sorry, man, I can't come in today. I'm hypnotized." By the way, to end your full-screen "trance," press the Escape key on your keyboard. To switch back from Full Screen to containing the Visualizer within the iTunes window, press Command-F (PC: Control-F) again.

Maximize Your Experience

If you have a fast computer, the Visualizer runs very quickly, with no jerkiness, stuttering, or other distractions. But if you're running iTunes on a computer that has a few miles on it, you might need to tweak the visuals a bit so they perform at their psychedelic best on your machine (after all, having smooth visuals is key to helping you achieve harmony of mind, body, and spirit—or some crap like that). That's why you need access to the Visualizer's options. When the Visualizer is "visualizing" within the iTunes window (not Full Screen mode), just look up where the Burn Disc button (which doubles as the Browse button, depending on where you are in iTunes) was, and you'll see that it has now become the Options button. Click on it, and the Visualizer Options dialog appears, in which you can display and/or slow down the frame rate and choose a faster (but rougher) onscreen display.

---

iTip

Okay, let's say you're sitting around trippin' on the Visualizer, and some friends come over. Have them stare directly into the center of the screen, tell them to focus their inner "chi" on that spot, and before long the spiritual epicenter of all that is cool will be revealed to them. Then, while they're focusing their inner chi, slowly move your hand over the keyboard and press the letter B, which makes the Apple logo fade into view, right in the center of the visuals, revealing the source of all that's cool. This is what's known in high-tech marketing jargon as "optimum logo placement." (Note: This feature may vary depending on your version of iTunes.)

Controlling the Visuals

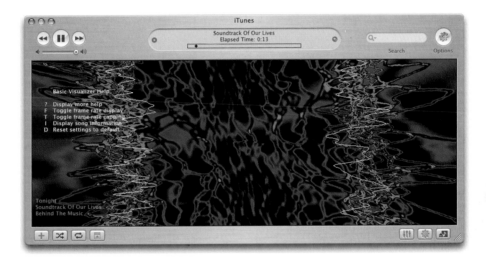

If you think the Visualizer is just a random set of visual randomness that's totally random, well, my friend, I have a startling revelation for you—it only "kind of" is. That's because you actually can control some aspects of the Visualizer while it's…well…visualizing. There are different one-key commands you can give while it's running to make it bend to your every whim. So what are these one-key wonders? While it's running, press the Question Mark (?) key and a list of basic commands will appear in the upper left-hand corner. Press the Question Mark key again for another list of options. To select an option, press the corresponding key on your keyboard.

---

iTip

When the Visualizer is running and a new song starts, the song's name, artist, album art (if present), and album name appear for a few moments in the bottom left-hand corner of the screen, then they slowly fade away (so as not to distract from the mind-bending array of patterns that will soon take over your screen, and perhaps even your life). However, if you'd like the song info not to fade away—to always be displayed—just click on the Options button—found in the upper right-hand corner of the iTunes window when the Visualizer is engaged—to bring up the Visualizer Options dialog. Now just turn on the checkbox for Always Display Song Info. Plus, if the song you're playing has accompanying album art, it's displayed, too.

Extreme Visuals

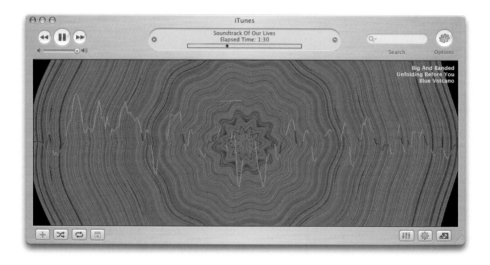

Here's the problem with visuals: There'll come a time when you're not getting a visual buzz anymore, and you need something stronger. So you press the letter Z and something cool happens. And that keeps you happy—for a while. But then you press it again, and again, and each time you press it, it gives you a different set of colors, and pretty soon you're pressing Z over and over again (notice the different configurations listed in the top-right corner of the iTunes window). But then that's not enough, and you press Q and your visuals just freak. But after a while, that just doesn't do it for you, and then eventually some friends talk you into trying the letter A, and I can't quite explain what pressing A does, but it's a stronger effect than Z or Q, and a lot of people get really strung out on A. That's the problem with the Visualizer. It's hard to stay just a casual user. You just keep pressing all the letters on your keyboard until you start to freak out.

---

iTip

After a while, pressing Z, Q, and even A—it's kid stuff, and you go looking for something more. You'll probably wind up on a website like soundspectrum.com, downloading third-party Visualizer plug-ins. Install the plug-ins by putting them in iTunes' Plug-ins folder (on the Mac, look inside your Home folder, in the Library, in the iTunes folder, and there you'll find the iTunes Plug-ins folder; on a Windows PC: in the Program folder, inside the iTunes folder, create a "Plug-ins" folder). Once you've installed them, go under iTunes' Visualizer menu and you'll see your plug-ins appear at the bottom of the menu.

Balancing the Volume between Songs

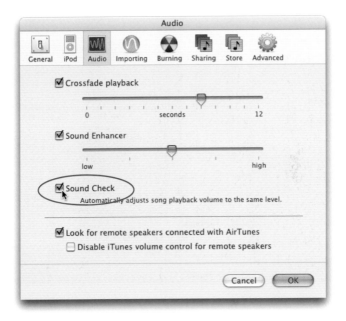

One of the perils of having an eclectic taste in music is that all music isn't recorded at the same volume. For example, if the first song in one of your playlists is "Concerto for Piano No. 21 in C Major, K 467, 2nd Movement, Andante," and the next song following that happens to be "I'm a Dog" by Kid Rock, I have to tell you that when "I'm a Dog" comes on, the volume (and sheer mass) of that song will send you scrambling for the Volume slider. If there were only some way that piano concertos and rock-rap could share the same volume setting. Ah, but there is: It's called Sound Check, and this iTunes preference setting lets you automatically balance the volume between songs just like your iPod does. Just go to iTunes Preferences (found under the iTunes menu on Mac, or the Edit menu on PC), and then click the Audio tab. Next, click the checkbox beside Sound Check to turn on iTunes' automatic volume balancing. So now when you glide from Frank Sinatra straight into Metallica, it'll be a smooth transition (at least in volume).

---

iTip

If you want to change the volume while you're playing a song, you don't have to grab the mouse and travel all the way up to the top-left corner—instead, you can adjust the volume right from your keyboard. To "crank up the jams," press Command-Up Arrow (PC: Control-Up Arrow) and to turn it back down (when the cops arrive), press Command-Down Arrow (PC: Control-Down Arrow).

Making Your Music Sound Better

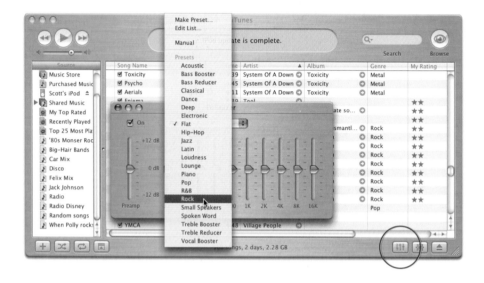

By default, the iTunes graphic equalizer (EQ) is set to flat, which is basically the same as setting the bass and treble sliders on your car stereo to the zero setting (flat is actually a good name for this state, because that's how it makes your stereo sound—flat). But you can use iTunes' built-in EQ to make your music sound dramatically better, and you don't have to understand how EQs work—presets based on the type of music you listen to are already built-in. Here's how to turn on iTunes' EQ: Click the EQ button at the bottom right of the iTunes window. At the top of the Equalizer dialog is a pop-up menu with presets—just choose the type of music you're listening to, and iTunes creates an EQ setting to make your music sound its best. If you want to create your own setting, just grab the sliders (bass on the left, midrange in the middle, and highs on the right) and make your own.

---

iTip

If you've created your own custom EQ setting (I created one for my laptop by starting with the R&B preset and then tweaking the Bass sliders), you can save it as your own custom preset. Once you've got your EQ set the way you want it, choose Make Preset from the presets pop-up menu in the Equalizer dialog. Name your preset in the resulting dialog. When you click OK, your preset is added to the presets pop-up menu and will appear in alphabetical order.

Individual EQ Settings by Song

I know what you're thinking: "Okay Scott, I set my overall EQ for iTunes to Rock, but some of my songs are R&B, some are classical, and some are dance. So my rock songs will sound great, but the rest are going to be EQ'd for rock, so they won't sound their best, right?" Right. That's why iTunes lets you assign EQs to individual songs, so you can assign an R&B EQ to R&B songs, and a Classical EQ to classical pieces. Here's how: Press Command-J (PC: Control-J) to bring up the View Options, then click the check-box beside Equalizer and an Equalizer column will appear in your iTunes window. To assign an EQ to a song, click on the song, then choose the EQ you want for that song from the EQ column's pop-up menu.

---

iTip

Applying EQ settings on a song-by-song basis can take some time, so here's a big timesaving shortcut: First, click on the Genre column to sort your songs by genre, then Shift-click the first song and the last song to select all the songs in that genre. Now Control-click (PC: Right-click) on any selected song, and in the contextual menu choose Get Info to bring up the Multiple Song Information dialog. Under the Equalizer Preset pop-up menu, choose an EQ preset and then click OK.

How Many Playlists Does a Song Appear In?

If you seem to be hearing a particular song an awful lot, it may be that the song appears in several different playlists, so you wind up changing playlists but still hearing that song again. Luckily, there's a slick way to find out exactly how many (and which) playlists a particular song appears in—just Control-click (PC: Right-click) on a song, and from the contextual menu that appears, go under Playlists to see a list of the playlists that contain that song. If you see quite a long list, you'll know why you've been hearing it so much.

---

iTip

Because you'll wind up having hundreds, maybe thousands, of songs in iTunes, and lots of different playlists, you'll be amazed at how easy it is to have more than one copy of a song (maybe with a slightly different name, or just in different playlists, or different versions of the same song). Luckily, there's a quick way to get rid of the duplicates—just go under the Edit menu and choose Show Duplicate Songs. This will bring up a list of all your duplicate songs. Then, if you have two (or more) copies, you can quickly click on the one(s) you want to delete and press the Delete (PC: Backspace) key on your keyboard.

Wirelessly Streaming Music to Your Stereo

If you have an AirPort Express Wireless 802.11g Base Station (and who doesn't these days?), you'll be able to connect it to your stereo either via a stereo link or optical cable (both sold separately). The minute iTunes sees an AirPort Express Base Station on your network and detects that you have something plugged into the line out port on it, you'll get a little pop-up menu in the lower right-hand corner of iTunes showing the name of your speakers (which you named in the AirPort Admin Utility when you set up your AirPort Express) and be able to choose it. Once speakers are chosen, when you choose a song and hit play, your music will automatically stream to your stereo or speakers connected to the AirPort Express. Keep in mind, though, that this is currently an either/or situation: You can either hear the music through your computer *or* through your AirPort Express, not both at the same time.

---

iTip

Once iTunes is playing, if you want to skip a song, repeat a song, pause a song, etc., you can do all of that without having to actually go into iTunes. That's because you can access these basic controls directly from the Dock (on a Mac) or the Taskbar (on a PC). On the Mac, just Control-click (or click–and–hold) on the iTunes icon in the Dock and a contextual menu of commands will appear. On a Windows PC, Right-click the iTunes icon in the Taskbar's Notification Area and a similar pop-up menu will appear.

Chapter Eleven
Add It On
iPod Accessories

The Bruces' song "Add It On" got the honor of being the name for this chapter about iPod accessories. Okay, granted, I'm not sure if it's exactly an "honor" to be chosen for a chapter name here, but it certainly beats getting nominated for a Grammy and then losing to Nelly (even though that never happened to "Add It On," but hey, it could've). Actually, now that you mention it, I wouldn't mind coming up with my own music award. Instead of a "Grammy" I could call it a "Scotty," and the award itself would either look like a small Scottish dog, or it could resemble James Doohan, who played Chief Engineer Montgomery "Scotty" Scott in the original *Star Trek* series. Now, if it were up to my friend Terry White (the tech editor for this book), he'd definitely name it a "Scotty" because he's a big *Star Trek* freak. There's a difference between a *Star Trek* freak and a *Star Trek* geek. You see, although Terry knows all the characters, plots, equipment, etc., by name and has even attended the occasional *Star Trek* convention, he claims he doesn't "dress up in costume" when he goes to the convention. He says that's "crossing the line." Yeah, I'm sure that's where the line is (wink, wink). I digress. Anyway, this chapter is about all the cool things you can add to your already cool iPod to make it so cool that it loses all its original coolness. Cool!

195

Bose SoundDock Digital Music System

If your goal is the best possible sound quality from a "designed-for-the-iPod" desktop speaker system, I'd have to say that the Bose SoundDock is the one, hands down. It's a great-looking system, and it even charges your iPod while it's in the Bose dock. It's not the smallest, and it's certainly not the cheapest at around $299, but when it comes to sheer quality of sound, it has no peer (it has peeps, but no peers). It works with any iPod that has a Dock connector on the bottom, plus it comes with a handy remote. You can find it at the Apple Store (online or in the mall), and you can learn more about it at bose.com.

JBL On Stage Speakers

If space and money are both in shorter supply, you're going to love JBL's On Stage speakers. It's a very slick-looking little setup, and your iPod looks great just sitting there in its Dock—even when it's not playing—and it doesn't take up nearly the desk space that the Bose system does. The On Stage can be used as a Dock when it's connected to your computer (with the same cable that comes with your iPod). It also has Audio In jacks, which makes it compatible with all iPods, and it can be used in a pinch with other things, including as a speaker system for your computer. However, as of the printing of this book, JBL's On Stage was not compatible with the iPod photo. The sound is pretty darn good, and the price is too, at around $199. You can find it at the Apple Store.

Altec Lansing inMotion iM3 Audio System

If you travel with your iPod and want a first-rate portable speaker system, or if you just want an incredibly small set of speakers, give the iM3 a look. Altec Lansing made the first portable audio system for the iPod—this is their third generation, and it keeps getting better and better (looks-wise and soundwise). By the way, the iM3 is for standard iPods—so that means it's not compatible with iPod photo. However, if you have an iPod mini, you can even go smaller with the iMmini Portable Audio System designed specifically for the iPod mini. Both systems operate on an AC power adapter or batteries. (*Note:* While operating on batteries, the system won't charge your iPod.) The inMotion system can also act as a Dock for connecting your iPod to your computer, and has an Audio In port, so it can be used as computer speakers. When this book went to press, the only place you could buy an iM3 was through Apple, but by the time you read this, you may be able to find it elsewhere. It sells for about $149, and you can find out more at the Apple Store (hey, that rhymes).

iPod Socks

This may well be the "lowest-tech" thing Apple has ever created, but people seem to really get a kick out of this collection of six different-colored socks that are designed to protect your iPod just like regular socks protect your feet (in other words, it's light on the protection aspect, heavy on the cuteness factor). You get all six colors and, of course, "one-size-fits-all," so they'll work with any model of iPod (after all, they're socks, for cryin' out loud). Find them at the Apple Store for around $29. Batteries not included (you didn't fall for that batteries line, did ya?—they're socks).

Colorize Your iPod

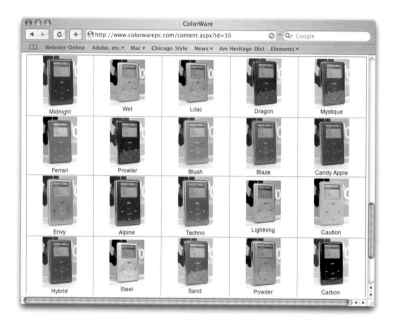

iPods and iPod photos come in basic white (well, except the U2 special edition, which is black). But if you really want your iPod in a different color, the folks at ColorWare Computer Products can hook you up. They specialize in colorizing iPods (and other computer stuff), and basically it works like this—you go to their website and pick a color (from their high-resolution photo samples), then you ship them your iPod, you send them around $49, and shortly thereafter you get a colorized iPod that looks like it came that way from the factory. They have 20 colors to choose from, and they can even create a custom color for you for about $99. Even if you're not longing for a color iPod, it's worth a stop by the site just to see what iPods in 20 different colors look like. They're at www.colorwarepc.com. (By the way, they only colorize regular iPods and iPod photo models—not iPod minis, which already come in five delicious colors.)

Marware iPod Armbands

If you want to literally wear your iPod mini when you're jogging or working out, you need an iPod armband. It holds your iPod mini firmly in place and keeps it within arm's length at all times. (Get, it? Arm's length. Okay, sorry about that one.) Apple sells its own brand of an armband (for the iPod mini only) for about $29 (and if you're really working up a sweat, it probably won't fit around your arm). But our favorite iPod mini armband is actually the Marware SportSuit Runabout, which provides some protection because your mini slips right into its thin case (but don't worry, you have full access to the Click Wheel and the screen at all times). Plus, it straps right to your wrist so you can wear your iPod mini like a watch. Best of all, it only costs a few cents more than Apple's. Find it at marware.com or wherever cool iPod stuff is sold.

Bose QuietComfort 2 Headphones

If you do a reasonable amount of air travel, you'll fall in love with the Bose Quiet-Comfort 2 Acoustic Noise Canceling Headphones. Besides just being great-sounding headphones (with great bass response), what makes this headphone set rock is its noise-canceling feature (which is absolutely amazing, and precisely why it works so well for air travel—it cancels out pretty much everything except the music). These headphones are almost legendary with frequent flyers, and using them with your iPod is the height of luxury, as evidenced by their price: about $299. Hey, I said they were great, I didn't say they were cheap. You can find them at Bose.com, on Apple.com, or wherever crazy-expensive headphones are sold.

Bang & Olufsen A8 Earphones

If you just want an outstanding pair of headphones (with a cool aluminum-and-black Euro look), and noise-canceling isn't a concern for you (you're not using them on flights or subway commutes), then check out Bang & Olufsen's A8 Earphones. They're lightweight, sound great, and they're less expensive (at about $159) than the Bose headphones (I say $159 like it's not a lot of money, but you know and I know that it is; it's just that compared to $299, it sounds like: "Hey, it's only $159!"). You can find these at Apple's online store or check them out at www.bang-olufsen.com/sw1612.asp.

Griffin iTalk Voice Recorder

If you'd like to turn your iPod into a voice recorder, check out Griffin's iTalk Voice Recorder. It simply plugs into the top of your iPod, and with its high-quality built-in microphone, you can use it for more than just making audio notes to yourself—you can record concerts, lectures, irate drive-thru restaurant staff—the mind reels. Plus, even though it's pretty darn small in size, it has its own built-in speaker that, for its size, delivers fairly decent sound. The only downside—it doesn't support the iPod mini. It sells for around $40, and you can find it at the Apple Store.

AirPort Express for Streaming iTunes

Apple's AirPort Express Base Station with AirTunes keeps on racking up national awards for its brilliant design as a wireless network device. But what you want it for is AirTunes, which gives you the ability to transmit your iTunes music wirelessly to your stereo (or just a pair of powered speakers) anywhere in your house, your office, hotel room—you name it. Think about it—your computer is in one room, but you're hearing your iTunes playlists on a stereo in another room of your house, and it's all wireless. Plus the setup is a no-brainer, and the whole thing works astonishingly well. You can buy it direct from Apple for around $129, and it's worth every penny! *Note:* As of the writing of this book, Keyspan has announced a wireless remote that plugs right into the USB port on the AirPort Express that allows you to play/pause, fast forward, and rewind your tracks without getting up and walking into the other room where your computer is located. Does it get any better than that?

Chapter Twelve

Get the
Lido Shuffle

How to Use
Apple's iPod shuffle

▶▶ When I heard Apple chose to name their new flash-memory-based iPod the "iPod shuffle," I was thrilled—mostly because it made my job of coming up with a song-based title for this chapter much easier. Two songs immediately came to mind: I could've gone with Queen's "Flash," and in most any situation going with a Queen song is a safe bet, as they're rather revered in the rock music world. However, the song "Flash" sucks. I'm sorry, but it does. You know it does. I know it does. If I played the song for my 8-year-old son (who thankfully doesn't use the word "sucks"), even he would find himself with no other choice but to use the word "sucks" as well, and I don't want to put him in that awkward position. So instead, I went with "Lido Shuffle," which is one of Boz Skaggs' coolest songs. Now, both of these songs are from the '80s, which automatically means they come with a measure of suckiness built right in, but we're simply going to overlook that, because it makes my job of naming the chapter even easier, and really, that's what this is all about: Making my life easy. Hey, speaking of easy (how's that for a lame segue), the iPod shuffle is fairly easy, thanks to the fact that it has no screen. When I first learned it had no screen, rather than calling it the iPod shuffle, I thought Apple should've named it something like iPod Blind or iPod in the Dark. Sadly, Apple never called me for my opinion. Or, I would've told them to name it iPod Bad Queen Song. That's probably why Apple didn't call.

Getting Songs into Your iPod shuffle

Getting songs into your iPod shuffle is a totally automated thing, and it couldn't be easier—just pull the little cap off the bottom of the iPod shuffle and plug it into a USB port on your computer (by the way, if you have a USB 2.0 port, plug it in there—the song transfers will go much faster). iTunes will automatically launch and a dialog will appear asking you to name your iPod shuffle. Then, iTunes will automatically choose exactly enough songs from your Library to fill your iPod shuffle with a random selection of songs (for my 512-MB iPod shuffle, iTunes chose 119 songs). This automatic filling of your iPod shuffle is called (no big surprise here) the Autofill feature.

---

iTip

To delete a song from your iPod shuffle, just click on the iPod shuffle icon that appears in the iTunes Source list (on the left side of the iTunes window) when your iPod shuffle is connected to your computer. When you do this, all the songs on your iPod shuffle will appear in the main window. To delete a song, just click on it and press the Delete (PC: Backspace) key on your keyboard.

Getting Songs You Actually Want

The first time you plug your iPod shuffle into your computer, iTunes just picks random songs from your Library and downloads those into your iPod shuffle until it's full. However, rather than using your Library, you probably will want to have it choose songs from one of your playlists instead (for example, when iTunes first downloaded songs into my iPod shuffle, it took along some Christmas songs. That'd be fine in December, but sadly, it was January). So, to have iTunes "autofill" from a playlist (rather than from your entire Library), just connect your iPod shuffle, then click on your iPod shuffle's icon in the Source list on the left side of the iTunes window. An Autofill panel will appear just below your main iTunes window. In the Autofill From pop-up menu, choose the playlist you want Autofill to pull songs from, and then click on the Autofill button on the left side of the window. As long as you have the Replace All Songs When Autofilling checkbox selected, iTunes will delete the songs that were on your iPod shuffle when you first plugged it in and replace them with songs from your currently selected playlist.

Turning On Your iPod shuffle

The switch for turning on the iPod shuffle is on the back. To turn the iPod on, slide the large switch down either one or two notches, revealing a green bar at the top. If you slide it down one notch to turn it on, it sets your iPod shuffle to play the songs in the same order they were imported. If you slide it down to the second notch, it will shuffle your songs and play them in a random order. Also, when you turn the iPod shuffle on, a green status light appears on the front, above the navigation buttons. (This green status light appears for just a few seconds, so if you really want to see it, flip your iPod over to the front after you turn it on.) To turn it off, just move the slider back up to the top (covering the green bar).

---

iTip

Want Autofill to show a bit more discretion when choosing songs for your iPod shuffle? Then make sure you turn on the Autofill checkbox for Choose Higher Rated Songs More Often. That way, when it randomly grabs the 120 (or 240) songs, it'll make sure that songs you've rated higher (the songs you like best) get chosen more often than the rest. So basically, you get a better random playlist.

Hearing the Songs on Your iPod shuffle

All right, your songs are on your iPod shuffle—now it's time to hear them. Plug the earbuds (which come with your iPod shuffle) into the headphone jack on the top of the iPod shuffle, and then press the Play/Pause button in the center of the circular Control Pad to hear a song. To pause (stop) the currently playing song, just press the center Play/Pause button again. If you don't like the currently playing song, you can skip past it by pressing the Fast Forward button on the right side of the circular Control Pad (needless to say, if you press the left button, it plays the previous song—that's why it's called the Previous/Rewind button). By the way, if you press-and-hold the Fast Forward button (rather than just pressing it once), the iPod shuffle fast-forwards through the currently playing song (and of course, holding down the Previous/Rewind button rewinds the song).

---

iTip

If at any time you want to jump back to the beginning of your playlist, just press the Play/Pause button three times really fast.

Adjusting the Volume

To turn the volume up, press the Plus (+) button on the top of the circular Control Pad.
To lower the volume, press the Minus (–) button at the bottom of the pad.

Manually Adding Songs to Your iPod shuffle

Source		▲	Song Name	Time	Artist	Genre	My Rating
Library		14	☑ Burnin' For You	4:30	Blue Oyster Cult		★★★
Party Shuffle		15	☑ Fly Me to the Moon (In Other W	2:28	Tom Jones	Vocal	
Music Store		16	☑ Dreamin'	4:11	Will to Power	Dance	
Purchased Music		17	☑ Runaway	3:52	Bon Jovi	Rock	★★★★★
Scott's iPod Shuffle		18	☑ honey for the bees	4:17	patti austin		
Car Mix		19	☑ Foolin'	4:33	Def Leppard	Rock	
My Top Rated		20	☑ Remote Control	4:00	The Reddings		★★★★★
Recently Played		21	☑ On The 4th Of July	3:25	James Taylor	Pop	★★★★
		22	☑ Sweetheart	4:11	Franke & The Knoc	Pop	

You don't have to use Autofill to get songs onto your iPod shuffle—just drag-and-drop the songs that you want from your iTunes Library directly onto the iPod shuffle icon that appears in the Source list (on the left side of the iTunes window) when your iPod shuffle is connected to your computer.

---

iTip

If you want the songs on your iPod shuffle to be in the exact same order as the ones in the playlist you're choosing to download, go to the Autofill panel at the bottom of the iTunes window and turn off the checkbox for Choose Songs Randomly. That way, songs aren't chosen at random, and instead will appear on your iPod shuffle in the same order as your selected playlist in iTunes.

Edit Your Shuffle Playlist without Connecting

Believe it or not, you can see, edit, add, and delete songs on your iPod shuffle, even when it's not connected to your computer—you just have to change one little preference setting, which keeps your iPod shuffle's list of songs visible even when you've disconnected it. That way, when you connect your iPod shuffle to your computer, it will update to reflect your changes. Here's how: While your iPod shuffle is connected to your computer, click on the iPod Options button that appears in the lower right-hand corner of the iTunes window. In the resulting dialog, choose Keep This iPod in the Source List. Now once you unplug your iPod shuffle, you'll notice its icon stays in the Source list on the left side of the iTunes window. To view the songs that are on your ejected iPod shuffle, just click on the iPod shuffle icon in iTunes. To add a song, just drag-and-drop it onto the icon. To delete a song, click on it in the iPod shuffle's song list and press the Delete (PC: Backspace) key on your keyboard. You can rearrange the order of songs and pretty much do everything you'd normally do to a playlist. Now the next time you plug in your iPod shuffle, it will update to reflect your changes. By the way, you can instantly see which songs are new and haven't yet been updated on your iPod shuffle, because a little circle icon appears to the left of the song's name (as shown above).

Fitting More Songs on Your iPod Shuffle

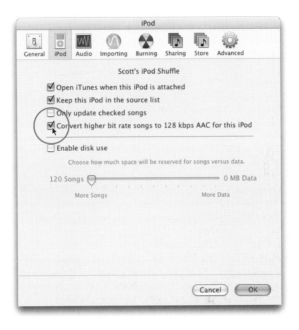

If you want to fit as many songs on your iPod shuffle as possible, you can have iTunes automatically convert your MP3, AIFF, and WAV files to AAC format when they're downloaded onto your iPod shuffle. AAC files are smaller in size, so you can fit more songs in the same space. To turn this feature on, plug your iPod shuffle into your computer, then click on the iPod Options button in the bottom right-hand corner of the iTunes window. When the dialog appears, turn on the checkbox for Convert Higher Bit Rate Songs to 128 kbps AAC for This iPod. Oh yeah, you don't have to worry about altering your original songs—it only converts songs as they're downloaded into your iPod shuffle; the songs in your iTunes Library remain untouched.

Finding Out How Much Battery Is Left

There's a battery status button on the back of the iPod shuffle. Press it and a battery indicator light (on the button itself) will give you a visual indicator of how much battery life is left. For example, if you press the button and the light is green, the battery is pretty well charged. If the light is yellow, the battery's getting low and before too long you should charge the battery by connecting your iPod shuffle to your computer's USB port or by putting your iPod shuffle in its Dock (if you bought one). If the light is red, you're "runnin' on empty" and soon you will experience "the sounds of silence." If you press the button and no light comes on at all, it's a brick—the battery's dead and you need to recharge before it can do anything—so plug that puppy into your computer's USB port for at least two hours, but to get a full charge, leave it plugged in for four.

---

iTip

When you plug your iPod shuffle into your computer's USB port, the status light (on the front of your iPod, near the top) will glow yellow, letting you know it's charging. When it's fully charged, it will turn green.

Locking the Buttons

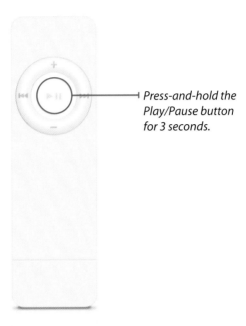

Press-and-hold the Play/Pause button for 3 seconds.

If you're tossing your iPod shuffle into your pocket, you might want to lock the buttons on the front, so your iPod shuffle doesn't accidentally change songs, pause, etc. To do that, just press-and-hold the Play/Pause button for 3 seconds. The status indicator light on the front will flash yellow three times, letting you know that things are safely locked down. If you click on a locked button, the yellow indicator will flash once to let you know that the buttons are locked. To unlock the Control Pad buttons, just hold down the same center Play/Pause button for 3 more seconds and the indicator light will flash green three times, letting you know you're unlocked and ready to rock (I know that sounds cheesy—I just couldn't help myself; it just felt so right).

Something Acting Funky? Try Resetting

If something seems to go wrong (your iPod shuffle won't play songs, etc.), you may need to reset your iPod shuffle. Just turn it off (by sliding the large switch on the back up to the OFF position) and leave it off for 5 seconds. Then turn it back on, and that should do the trick.

---

iTip

Okay, this tip doesn't really belong in the iPod shuffle chapter—it really belongs in the iTunes Music Store chapter, but I've got the space here, so here it be. If you like a particular artist, you can be emailed when he or she adds a new song (or album) to the iTunes Music Store. This feature is called Artist Alert, and to sign up for it, just do a search for your favorite artist, click on any album art to launch that album's page, and then to the right of the main album art, click on Add Artist Alert. It's as easy as that.

Storing Files on Your iPod shuffle

Besides storing music, you can easily configure your iPod shuffle to hold non-audio files as well, so basically it can "double" as a flash drive. Here's how: Once your iPod shuffle is connected to your computer, in iTunes click on your iPod shuffle in the Source list, and then click on the iPod Options button in the bottom right-hand corner of the window. Turn on the checkbox for Enable Disk Use, then move the slider below the checkbox to decide how many songs you want versus how much data you want to be able to store. (As you move the slider, you'll get live feedback showing how much data space versus how many songs you're able to store.) Click OK and your iPod shuffle will appear on your desktop (on a Mac) or as an available drive on a Windows PC. Now you can just drag-and-drop files right onto it, treating it as though it's a portable flash drive. *Note:* To protect the data on your iPod shuffle, always click on the Eject button in iTunes before you disconnect it (see the next page).

When Do You Need to Eject the iPod shuffle?

If you're just using the iPod shuffle to store songs, you don't need to do anything special when it's time to disconnect your iPod—just be sure not to unplug it while it's updating. (An easy way to know if it's safe to unplug is to look up at the status display at the top center of the iTunes window. If iTunes is done updating your iPod shuffle, the status display will show: "iPod Update is Complete. OK to Disconnect.") However, if you're using your iPod shuffle to store both songs and data (other non-audio files from your computer), you'll first need to ensure that your iPod is done updating, and then you'll need to click on the Eject button, which appears in the lower right-hand corner of the iTunes window. When you do this, iTunes "unmounts" your iPod shuffle, so it's safe to remove your iPod shuffle from your computer without the risk of damaging data.

Appendix

Recommended Dose

A Peek at My Own Personal, Ultra-Secret, Yet Surprisingly Way-Cool Playlists

Okay, this last part isn't really a chapter. It's too short to be a chapter, and it really doesn't tell you how to use your iPod. So what is it? Some ideas to help you build your musical collection. And to that end I'm going to pull aside the veil of secrecy, remove the cone of silence, and openly share some of my very own playlists, thereby stripping away any pretense and baring my musical soul to you, my esteemed reader (and contributor to my son's college fund). Basically, what I did was gather some of my playlists and publish them as iMixes on the iTunes Music Store (samples follow, and the ITMS links to them appear on each page). If you want to hear a 30-second preview of any of my recommended songs, you can do that right from my iMixes, and if you like one of those songs, you can buy it right there, too. Now, I don't get any kickbacks or royalties from Apple—but if you download one (or all) of these songs (yes, just one click and you can buy the entire playlist), there will be a time when you and I are both playing the exact same song at the exact same time—and from that moment on there will be a connection, a sacred bond between us that can never be broken. Oh yeah, I asked my tech editor, Terry White, to share one of his playlists too; but if you buy his songs, there's no bond. Sorry, that's just the way he is. By the way, the chapter title came from a song by Rico, from his album *Violent Silences*. If I had made that album, I would've named it "Abbey Road."

223

Scott's Big Hair Rock Mix Playlist

A mix of my favorite 1980s and early '90s commercial rock songs

I published these songs as an iMix on the iTunes Music Store. You can find this list (and buy the songs online) at **http://phobos.apple.com/WebObjects/MZStore.woa/ wa/viewPublishedPlaylist?id=52478.**

Scott's '80s Club Dance Mix Playlist

What we danced to in the clubs back then, in our sport coats with the sleeves rolled

I published these songs as an iMix on the iTunes Music Store. You can find this list (and buy the songs online) at **http://phobos.apple.com/WebObjects/MZStore.woa/wa/ viewPublishedPlaylist?id=166339.**

Scott's All-Around Feel-Good Mix

Songs to make you smile when you're already in a really good mood

I published these songs as an iMix on the iTunes Music Store. You can find this list (and buy the songs online) at **http://phobos.apple.com/WebObjects/MZStore.woa/wa/viewPublishedPlaylist?id=166376.**

Jordan's Radio Disney–Like Playlist

The songs my 8-year-old son likes on AM Radio Disney

I published these songs as an iMix on the iTunes Music Store. You can find this list (and buy the songs online) at **http://phobos.apple.com/WebObjects/MZStore.woa/wa/viewPublishedPlaylist?id=166351.**

Terry's Top 25

My tech editor Terry White's top 25 favorite songs—Terry's a freak

◄ ►	🏠 > iMix > iMixes by this user > Terry's Top 25			Account: Sign In

Terry's Top 25

See all iMixes by this user ➜
Tell a friend ➜
Total Songs: 25
$24.75 BUY ALL SONGS
How do I make an iMix? ➜

Rating

○ ★★★★★
○ ★★★★
○ ★★★
○ ★★
○ ★

Submit

iMix Notes

25 of my all time favorites!

	Song Name	Time	Artist	Album	Price	
1	Baby Boy	4:04	Beyoncé & Sean ... ➜	Dangerously in ... ➜	$0.99	BUY SONG
2	Butterflies	4:29	Floetry ➜	Floacism "Live" ➜	$0.99	BUY SONG
3	Fallin'	3:30	Alicia Keys ➜	Songs in A Minor ➜	$0.99	BUY SONG
4	Keep Looking	5:24	Sade ➜	Stronger Than P... ➜	$0.99	BUY SONG
5	Emotion	3:56	Destiny's Child ➜	Survivor ➜	$0.99	BUY SONG
6	Emotional Rollercoaster (Album V...	3:17	Vivian Green ➜	Emotional Roller... ➜	$0.99	BUY SONG
7	Billie Jean	4:52	Michael Jackson ➜	Thriller (Special ... ➜	$0.99	BUY SONG
8	Take You Out	3:25	Luther Vandross ➜	Luther Vandross ➜	$0.99	BUY SONG
9	To Zion	6:09	Lauryn Hill & Sa... ➜	The Miseducatio... ➜	$0.99	BUY SONG
10	Dangerously in Love 2	4:53	Beyoncé ➜	Dangerously in ... ➜	$0.99	BUY SONG
11	Pearls	4:35	Sade ➜	The Best of Sade... ➜	$0.99	BUY SONG
12	You	4:42	Janet Jackson ➜	The Velvet Rope ➜	$0.99	BUY SONG
13	Foolish [EXPLICIT]	3:47	Ashanti ➜	Ashanti ➜	$0.99	BUY SONG
14	Say Yes (Intro)	1:04	Floetry ➜	Floacism "Live" ➜	$0.99	BUY SONG
15	Say Yes	5:56	Floetry ➜	Floacism "Live" ➜	$0.99	BUY SONG
16	If Only for One Night	5:58	Luther Vandross ➜	Live at Radio Cit... ➜	$0.99	BUY SONG
17	Morning	0:31	Janet Jackson ➜	Janet. ➜	$0.99	BUY SONG
18	Nite and Day	4:03	Al B. Sure! ➜	In Effect Mode ➜	$0.99	BUY SONG
19	Fly	3:52	Al Jarreau ➜	All Fly Home ➜	$0.99	BUY SONG
20	Shake Your Body (Down to the Gr...	8:00	The Jacksons ➜	Destiny ➜	$0.99	BUY SONG
21	Memory Lane (Single)	3:30	Minnie Riperton ➜	Capitol Gold: Th... ➜	$0.99	BUY SONG
22	In the Stone	4:50	Earth, Wind & Fire ➜	I Am ➜	$0.99	BUY SONG
23	Gloria	5:36	Enchantment ➜	If You're Ready..... ➜	$0.99	BUY SONG
24	Let's Get It Started (Spike Mix) [B...	3:39	Black Eyed Peas ➜	Elephunk ➜	$0.99	BUY SONG
25	Back in the Day	4:46	Erykah Badu ➜	Worldwide Unde... ➜	$0.99	BUY SONG

Terry published these songs as an iMix on the iTunes Music Store. You can find this list (and buy the songs online) at **http://phobos.apple.com/WebObjects/MZStore. woa/wa/viewPublishedPlaylist?id=165878.**

Where to Go for More Song Ideas

Want more song ideas? Check out Cliff Colby's very cool The iPod Playlist Book

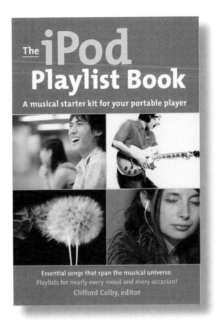

You can find Cliff's book at Amazon.com, BN.com, peachpit.com, or in bookstores. (ISBN 0-321-30469-1; 160 pages; $14.99. Published by Peachpit Press.) By the way, Cliff asked me to contribute a playlist for his book, so I contributed a playlist called "Songs guaranteed to pack the dance floor." Now, how would I know which songs make people shake their booties with wild abandon? You'll have to buy the book to find out the scandalous, disturbing, and otherwise shocking real-world inside story behind my experience on this topic. (Hint: Just in case you were wondering—I wasn't a DJ.)

Index

GRIFFIN & iPod In Perfect Harmony

iTripblack
FM Transmitter for all iPods

- Transmit audio from your iPod to any FM radio
- Powered from iPod - no batteries necessary
- Controlled directly from the iPod
- Uses any frequency from 87.7 to 107.9

iTalk
Voice Recorder for iPods

- Turns your iPod into a portable voice recorder and playback machine
- Pass-through jack on top for headphones or separate external microphone
- Built-in omnidirectional microphone and high quality 20mm speaker for playback

iTrip
FM Transmitter for all iPods

- Transmit audio from your iPod to any FM radio
- Powered from iPod - no batteries necessary
- Controlled directly from the iPod
- Uses any frequency from 87.7 to 107.9

PowerPod
Auto Charger for all iPods

- Works with all iPod models
- Includes removable Dock-to-FireWire cable
- Charge your iPod while playing your music
- Fused to protect against power surges

iTrip mini
FM Transmitter for iPod mini

- The only FM transmitter designed exclusively for the iPod mini
- Transmit audio from your iPod mini to any FM radio
- Powered from iPod mini - no batteries necessary
- Controlled directly from the iPod mini
- Uses any frequency from 87.7 to 107.9

EarJams
Enhance The Sound & Comfort of your iPod Earbuds

- Deliver massive bass and improved sound
- Enhance the comfort and fit of your iPod earbuds
- Package includes carrying case and adjustable earpads

iBeam
Keychain Flashlight & Laser Pointer For iPods

- Turns your iPod into a laser pointer or a flashlight
- Powered by the iPod - no batteries necessary
- Includes snap-on keychain caps

PodPod
Cup Holder Insert for iPod & iPod mini

- Won't scratch or mar iPod's surface
- Puts iPod at an easy-to-view angle
- Allows for excellent iTrip placement close to a car's antenna
- Holds iPod, iPod mini, or cell phone